The Corporation: Growth, Diversification and Mergers

FUNDAMENTALS OF PURE AND APPLIED ECONOMICS

Continued on inside back cover

The Corporation: Growth, Diversification and Mergers

Dennis C. Mueller
University of Maryland, USA

A volume in the Theory of the Firm and Industrial Organization section
edited by

Alexis Jacquemin
Université Catholique de Louvain, Belgium

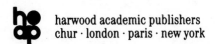
harwood academic publishers
chur · london · paris · new york

© 1987 by Harwood Academic Publishers GmbH
Poststrasse 22, 7000 Chur, Switzerland

Harwood Academic Publishers

Post Office Box 197
London WC2E 9PX
England

58, rue Lhomond
75005 Paris
France

Post Office Box 786
Cooper Station
New York, NY 10276
United States of America

Library of Congress Cataloging-in-Publication Data

Mueller, Dennis C.
  The corporation: growth, diversification and mergers.

  (Fundamentals of pure and applied economics; vol. 16.
Theory of the firm and industrial organization section,
ISSN 0191-1708)
  Includes index.
  1. Corporations. I. Title. II. Series: Fundamentals
of pure and applied economics; vol. 16. III. Series:
Fundamentals of pure and applied economics. Theory of
the firm and industrial organization section.
HD2731.M75   1987   338.7'4   86-19553
ISBN 3-7186-0357-8

Contents

Introduction to the Series

Drawing on a personal network, an economist can still relatively easily stay well informed in the narrow field in which he works, but to keep up with the development of economics as a whole is a much more formidable challenge. Economists are confronted with difficulties associated with the rapid development of their discipline. There is a risk of "balkanisation" in economics, which may not be favorable to its development.

Fundamentals of Pure and Applied Economics has been created to meet this problem. The discipline of economics has been subdivided into sections (listed inside). These sections include short books, each surveying the state of the art in a given area.

Each book starts with the basic elements and goes as far as the most advanced results. Each should be useful to professors needing material for lectures, to graduate students looking for a global view of a particular subject, to professional economists wishing to keep up with the development of their science, and to researchers seeking convenient information on questions that incidentally appear in their work.

Each book is thus a presentation of the state of the art in a particular field rather than a step-by-step analysis of the development of the literature. Each is a high-level presentation but accessible to anyone with a solid background in economics, whether engaged in business, government, international organizations, teaching, or research in related fields.

Three aspects of *Fundamentals of Pure and Applied Economics* should be emphasized:

—First, the project covers the whole field of economics, not only theoretical or mathematical economics.

—Second, the project is open-ended and the number of books is not predetermined. If new interesting areas appear, they will generate additional books.

—Last, all the books making up each section will later be grouped to constitute one or several volumes of an Encyclopedia of Economics.

The editors of the sections are outstanding economists who have selected as authors for the series some of the finest specialists in the world.

J. Lesourne   *H. Sonnenschein*

The Corporation: Growth, Diversification and Mergers

DENNIS C. MUELLER†

University of Maryland, USA

INTRODUCTION

Adam Smith's famous discussion of the organization of production in a pin factory articulated the advantages of the division of labor, the economic gains from specialization and large scale production. But Adam Smith expressed considerable skepticism concerning the relative efficiency of that particular form of business organization we now name the corporation, in which ownership and management are separated (1937, p. 700). Yet it has been this organizational form that has come to rule the day and on a scale and scope that the Scottish sage could hardly have imagined.

In 1980, there were 2,711,000 corporations in the United States, more than one corporation for every 100 Americans. Between 1920 and 1980 there was an eightfold increase in the number of corporations (see Table I). Moreover, as a group they accounted for nearly 90 percent of business receipts in 1980, a fraction that is up from $\frac{2}{3}$ in 1945.[1]

Not only do corporations as a group account for a large fraction of economic activity, but the biggest of these take on a scale that makes the word "firm" seem a misnomer. The total assets of

† Financial support for this research was received from the Thyssen Foundation of West Germany. Helpful comments on the first draft were received from Paul Geroski, Alexis Jacquemin, and Steven Klepper.
[1] See the *Statistical Abstract* (1984, p. 532); and *Historical Statistics, Colonial Times to 1970*, Part II, p. 911.

1

TABLE I

Number of US corporations, by industrial division: 1920–1980 (thousands)

	1920	1930	1940	1950	1960	1970	1980
Total active corps.	346[1]	463	473	629	1,141	1,665	2,711
Agriculture, forestry, and fishing	9	10	8	8	17	37	81
Mining	18	12	10	9	13	15	26
Construction	10	19	16	28	72	139	272
Manufacturing	78	92	86	116	166	198	243
Transportation and public utilities	21	22	22	26	44	67	111[3]
Wholesale and retail trade	79[2]	109	123	194	335	516	800
Finance, insurance, and real estate	79	137	143	172	334	406	493
Services	18	38	41	55	121	281	671

[1] Includes inactive corporations.
[2] Includes nonallocable corporations (about 25).
[3] Includes private utilities.
Sources: *Historical Statistics, Colonial Times to 1970,* Part II, p. 914. Table titled "Number of Corporations, by Industrial Division: 1916 to 1970." *1984 Statistical Abstract,* p. 533, Table No. 890, "Number of Returns, Receipts, and Net Income by Industry and Type of Business: 1980."

American Telephone and Telegraph Company in 1982 (prior to its break-up) were nearly $150 billion, a figure which exceeded the total personal wealth in the 6-state New England area. General Motors, the second largest U.S. industrial corporation, had an employment in 1983 of 691,000 workers, about the population of South Dakota. The third largest industrial corporation, Mobile Oil, had 1983 sales equal to the GNP of Denmark. The sales of the 20 largest U.S. corporations are listed in Table II. The sales of the 99 largest foreign mining and manufacturing companies are listed in Table III. Large size is a corporate attribute around the world.

This fact is further illustrated by the figures on aggregate concentration. The 100 largest manufacturing corporations in the United States accounted for nearly 50 percent of all manufacturing assets (see Table IV). Similar levels of concentration are observed in other countries, as for example the United Kingdom (Table IV).

This essay describes the process by which corporations grow to reach such historically unprecedented sizes. It traces the develop-

TABLE II
Top 20 industrial corporations, 1983

Rank	Company	Sales ($ millions)
1	Exxon	88,561
2	General Motors	74,582
3	Mobil	54,607
4	Ford Motor	44,455
5	International Business Machines	40,180
6	Texaco	40,068
7	E. I. Du Pont de Nemours	35,378
8	Standard Oil (Indiana)	27,635
9	Standard Oil (California)	27,342
10	General Electric	26,797
11	Gulf Oil	26,581
12	Atlantic Richfield	25,147
13	Shell Oil	19,678
14	Occidental Petroleum	19,116
15	U.S. Steel	16,869
16	Phillips Petroleum	15,249
17	Sun	14,730
18	United Technologies	14,669
19	Tenneco	14,353
20	ITT	14,155

Source: *Fortune*, April 30, 1984, p. 276.

ment of a representative corporation from birth to maturity. Special attention is devoted to roles of diversification and merger in the corporate growth process. In Section III, we contrast the growth and development of the large corporation with the evolution of capitalism. But we begin by reviewing the premises of the analysis.

TABLE III
The largest foreign mining and manufacturing companies

	Revenue[1] ($ millions)	Net income ($ millions)	Assets ($ millions)	Corporate headquarters	Industry	Employees (thousands)
1. Royal Dutch/Shell Group	80,610	4,178	70,766	Netherlands/United Kingdom	Energy	156.0
2. British Petroleum Co. Plc.	49,231	1,564	39,419	United Kingdom	Energy	131.6
3. ENI-Ente Nazionale Idrocarburi	25,166	−915	26,713	Italy	Energy	140.0
4. Toyota Motor Corp.	21,470	920	13,431	Japan	Automotive	57.8
5. Pemex-Petroleos Mexicanos	20,756	6,685	38,804	Mexico	Energy	160.0
6. Unilever	20,306	579	11,211	Netherlands/United Kingdom	Consumer Goods	267.0
7. National Iranian Oil Co.	19,000[E]	NA	NA	Iran	Energy	NA
8. VEBA Group	18,859	146	11,969[5]	Germany	Energy	77.3
9. Hitachi Ltd.	18,479	707	20,521	Japan	Elec. Equipment	161.5
10. TOTAL Group-Francaise des Petroles	18,314	102	10,992	France	Energy	43.6
11. Elf-Aquitaine Group	17,587	488	17,994	France	Energy	75.5
12. Matsushita Electric Industrial Co.	16,745	767	14,746	Japan	Elec. Equipment	124.8
13. Nissan Motor Co. Ltd.	16,309	419	13,418	Japan	Automotive	59.0[6]
14. NV Philips Lamp	16,181	27[7]	15,584[7]	Netherlands	Elec. Equipment	343.0
15. Petrobas-Petroleo Brasileiro SA	16,085	481	14,038	Brazil	Energy	56.7
16. Siemons Group	15,730	296	15,313	Germany	Elec. Equipment	313.0
17. Volkswagen Group	15,701	−51	10,571	Germany	Automotive	232.0
18. Daimler-Benz Group	15,668	369	9,038	Germany	Automotive	184.6
19. Nippon Oil Co. Ltd.	15,243	87	6,665	Japan	Energy	11.6
20. Petroleos de Venezuela SA	14,897	1,764	24,589	Venezuela	Energy	44.5

21.	BASF Group	14,824	203	8,030	Germany	Chemicals & Drug	114.1
22.	Bayer Group	14,623	296	10,971	Germany	Chemicals & Drug	174.8
23.	Hoechst Group	14,565	288	9,739	Germany	Chemicals & Drug	179.8
24.	Renault Group	14,469	−212	10,800	France	Automotive	219.8
25.	Fiat Group	13,986	NA	18,393	Italy	Automotive	243.1
26.	Nestle	13,312	601	9,401	Switzerland	Food Processing	140.4
27.	Volvo Group	12,972	239	6,687	Sweden	Automotive	71.5
28.	Imperial Chemical Ind. Plc.	12,524	573	11,055	United Kingdom	Chemicals & Drug	117.9
29.	Kuwait Petroleum Corp.	12,237	1,075	13,800	Kuwait	Energy	14.0[6]
30.	Mitsubishi Heavy Ind. Ltd.	11,943	99	17,362	Japan	Industrial Equip.	96.6
31.	Idemitsu Kasan Co. Ltd.[6]	11,885	137	6,932	Japan	Energy	7.0
32.	Nippon Steel Corp.	11,602	143	15,847	Japan	Steel	74.2
33.	Peugeot Group SA	11,350	−328	8,750[5]	France	Automotive	203.0
34.	Thyssen Group	11,306	−222	6,754	Germany	Steel	139.2
35.	Honda Motor Co. Ltd.	10,000	403	6,114	Japan	Automotive	51.4
36.	Ölag-Österreichische Industrie Verwaltungs AG	9,831	0	3,521	Austria	Metals	106.6
37.	RWE Group	9,769	174	11,241	Germany	Energy	70.4
38.	Toshiba Corp.	9,619	154	9,778	Japan	Elec. Equipment	103.0
39.	NV Nederlandse Gasunie	9,522	28	2,539	Netherlands	Energy	1.8
40.	Indian Oil Corp. Ltd.	9,308	122	3,129	India	Energy	27.9
41.	Petrolina SA	8,719	276	5,583	Belgium	Energy	21.0
42.	National Coal Board	8,245	−811	8,139	United Kingdom	Energy	268.0
43.	Cie Generale d'Electricite	8,196	53	10,111	France	Elec. Equipment	148.7
44.	INH-Instituto Nacional de Hidrocarburos	8,040P	82P	7,237[5]	Spain	Energy	23.8
45.	General Electric Co. Plc.	7,734	657	6,772	United Kingdom	Elec. Equipment	178.0
46.	Saint-Gobain	7,532	54P	6,733	France	Building Products	134.0
47.	Le Groupe Thomson	7,397	−150E	8,082[5]	France	Elec. Equipment	128.6
48.	Maruzen Oil Co. Ltd.	7,298	43	3,958	Japan	Energy	3.0[6]
49.	Rio Tinto-Zinc Corp. Plc.	7,298	170	11,082	United Kingdom	Metals	73.8
50.	Ruhrkohle	7,199	−7	5,434	Germany	Mining	130.0
51.	CIBA-GEIGY Group	7,022	388	9,053[7]	Switzerland	Chemicals & Drug	79.2

TABLE III

	Revenue[1] ($ millions)	Net income ($ millions)	Assets ($ millions)	Corporate headquarters	Industry	Employees (thousands)
52. Montedison Group	7,018	-212	6,445	Italy	Chemicals & Drug	72.8
53. NVDSM	6,928	57	3,346	Netherlands	Chemicals & Drug	27.9
54. Krupp Group	6,765	NA	3,716	Germany	Steel	69.3
55. Gutehoffnungshötte Group	6,434	-35[6]	4,799[6]	Germany	Industrial Equip.	79.6
56. Nippon Kokan KK	6,265	104	10,641	Japan	Steel	38.6
57. Mitsubishi Electric Corp.	6,240	140	5,935	Japan	Electric Equip.	64.4
58. Mazda Motor Corp.	6,066	114	3,509	Japan	Automotive	28.7
59. Grand Metropolitan Plc.	6,050	325	5,216	United Kingdom	Consumer Goods	136.3
60. NEC Corp.	5,781	132	6,897	Japan	Elec. Equipment	73.1
61. Rhône-Poulenc Group	5,657	13	4,719	France	Chemicals & Drug	82.0
62. Robert Bosch Group	5,621	NA	4,115[5]	Germany	Automotive	109.7
63. Nippon Mining Co. Ltd.	5,610	20	4,062	Japan	Energy	6.1
64. Mitsubishi Oil Co. Ltd.	5,518	93	3,419	Japan	Energy	2.7[6]
65. Mannesmann Group	5,512	30	3,747	Germany	Industrial Equip.	104.8
66. BMW-Bayerische Motoren Werke	5,493	113[6]	1,910[6]	Germany	Automotive	50.2
67. Sumitomo Metal Industries Ltd.	5,491	130	9,044	Japan	Steel	29.0[6]
68. British Steel Corp.	5,402	-1,452	5,174	United Kingdom	Steel	94.8
69. Gaz de France	5,337	-313	5,493	France	Utility	29.1
70. Chinese Petroleum Corp.[6]	5,333	431	4,025	Taiwan	Energy	19.5
71. Alcan Aluminium Ltd.	5,305	58	6,600	Canada	Metals	70.3
72. Akzo Group	5,285	150	3,529	Netherlands	Chemicals & Drug	66.3
73. Toa Nenryo Kogyo KK	5,258	166	3,428	Japan	Energy	2.4[6]
74. Ruhrgas	5,219	137	2,624	Germany	Energy	4.3
75. Michelin Group	5,196	-281	7,690[5]	France	Automotive	120.0
76. BL Plc.	5,189	-230	3,633	United Kingdom	Automotive	103.2

77. BBC-Brown Boveri Group	5,077	14[6]	1,941[6]	Switzerland	Elec. Equipment	90.6
78. Kobe Steel Ltd.[5]	4,884	48	7,030	Japan	Steel	30.7[6]
79. Daikyo Oil Co. Ltd.	4,850E	42	2,216	Japan	Energy	2.0[6]
80. Mitsubishi Chemical Industries	4,823	−15	4,509[5]	Japan	Chemicals & Drug	8.5[6]
81. Sanyo Electric Co. Ltd.	4,811	142	4,398	Japan	Elec. Equipment	22.8
82. Sony Corp.	4,671	124	5,267	Japan	Elec. Equipment	42.7
83. Dalgety Plc.	4,592	52	1,301	United Kingdom	Food Processing	21.2
84. Kawasaki Steel Corp.[6]	4,580	75	7,467	Japan	Steel	29.3
85. Thorn EMI Plc.	4,540	68	2,715	United Kingdom	Elec. Equipment	91.5
86. AEG Telefunken Group	4,515	22	3,218	Germany	Elec. Equipment	77.0
87. Canadian Wheat Board	4,443	NA	3,482	Canada	Grain	0.6
88. Degussa AG	4,422	36	1,413	Germany	Metals	21.4
89. Charbonnages de France	4,400E	−300E	4,700E	France	Energy	71.0
90. Kajima Corp.	4,360	73	4,863	Japan	Construction	15.6
91. Taiyo Fishery Co. Ltd.	4,295	−12	1,893	Japan	Food Processing	4.9[6]
92. Broken Hill Proprietary Co. Ltd.	4,290	217	6,825	Australia	Steel	56.1
93. Usinor	4,264	−715	4,912	France	Steel	54.0
94. Neste Oy	4,260	11	2,286	Finland	Energy	7.2
95. Showa Oil Co. Ltd.[6]	4,200E	35E	2,226[5]	Japan	Energy	1.8
96. Electrolux Group	4,193	112	2,941	Sweden	Elec. Equipment	88.8
97. Associated British Foods Plc.	4,127	257	2,048	United Kingdom	Food Processing	81.4
98. Norsk Hydro	4,080	154	3,227	Norway	Energy	18.8
99. Taisei Corp.	4,055	55	4,116	Japan	Construction	12.3

[1] Revenue figures are for group or consolidated operations and exclude excise taxes and duties.

[2] As of December 31, 1983.

[3] Combined market value.

[4] Not publicly traded.

[5] Figures from latest available balance sheet.

[6] Not fully consolidated.

[7] Based on current cost accounting.

NA: Not Available, E: Estimated, P: Preliminary.

General Note: Revenue and net income are converted at an average rate of exchange for the fiscal year-end rate. For companies with February and March fiscal year-ends, 1983 figures are used when more current data are not available.

TABLE IV

Largest U.S. manufacturing corporations—percent share of assets held: 1955–1982*

Corporation rank group	1955	1960	1963	1970	1973	1974	1975	1976	1977	1978	1979	1980	1981	1982
100 Largest	44.3	46.4	46.5	48.5	44.7	44.4	45.0	45.4	45.9	45.5	46.1	46.7	46.8	47.7
200 Largest	53.3	56.1	56.7	60.4	56.9	56.7	57.5	58.0	58.5	58.3	59.0	59.7	60.0	60.8

* Prior to 1970, excludes newspapers. Data prior to 1974 not strictly comparable with later years.
Source: 1984 Statistical Abstract, p. 538.

Largest manufacturing enterprises—percent share of net output, United Kingdom: 1909–1970

Corporation rank group	1909	1924	1935	1949	1953	1958	1963	1968	1970	1976
100 Largest	16[a]	22[a]	24	22	27	32	37[b]	41	39.8	41.8

[a] Approximate figures.
[b] Includes steel companies; reduced to $36\frac{1}{2}$ percent approximately if steel companies are excluded.
Source: S. J. Prais, *The Evolution of Giant Firms in Britain*, Cambridge: Cambridge University Press, 1981.

Part I

ENTREPRENEURIAL CAPITALISM

A. Premises

One of the most important intellectual developments in economics of the last two decades has been to go inside the black box of the corporate firm. A major theme of this literature has been the importance of transaction costs and transaction costs savings in explaining the nature of the firm, its organizational structure, and its evolution.[2] The properties of various hierarchical control structures are examined with respect to their relative efficiency at transmitting information, coordinating the activities of the factory owners, and producing proper incentives for all of the corporation's team members to contribute to the joint-productive activity. The evolution of the corporate firm is described largely in terms of the relative efficiency of differing corporate structures in coping with their internal and external environments.

The explanatory power of the transactions costs approach hinges on the tautness of the external economic environment in which corporations operate. If product markets are highly competitive, then managers must adopt the most efficient organizational forms or their companies will not survive. If the market for corporate control is highly competitive, then managers must adopt the most efficient organizational forms or they, the managers, will not survive even though their firms might. I shall assume throughout this essay that the corporation operates in an environment that is not so Darwinianly competitive so as to force a single, most efficient evolutionary pattern on each corporation. Rather, I posit the existence of enough long-lived monopoly power, enough transaction costs in eliminating monopoly and sufficient transaction costs in removing managers who deviate from the efficiency path to allow managers to

---

[2] For surveys of this literature, see Williamson (1979, 1981); Caves (1980).

select from among a variety of patterns of corporate growth. I presume the viability of a wide range of corporate development scenarios within the survivorship boundaries market forces establish.

These presumptions require empirical justification, which shall be provided below. Pockets of market power persist for considerable periods. The market for corporate control is not one in which more efficient managements are selected to replace less efficient ones. In part, however, these assumptions are justified because the scale of the corporation's domain has grown to such a magnitude that it is no longer legitimate to study the corporation's development only in terms of economic environmental forces operating upon and shaping the corporation's development. When a Chrysler in the United States or an AEG in West Germany face bankruptcy, the issues regarding its future are not resolved solely on the basis of its ability "to meet the market test." The large corporation is capable of shaping its environment by exerting pressure upon political and legal institutions. Should the corporation wish to evolve within an economic environment that is less hostile, it is capable of bringing about institutional changes that facilitate the pattern of development it has chosen. The development of corporate capitalism is best viewed as an interaction between the corporation's social, legal, and economic environment and the corporation. Institutions are as much the product of corporate and other social pressures as corporate development forms are a product of market institutions (Goldberg, 1974).

It is ironic, perhaps, that the existence of some Darwinian slack in the economic environment is a necessary assumption to warrant the economist's interest in transaction cost efficiencies. Were the economic environment so ruthless as to quickly weed out all inefficient organizational structures, one could treat the firm as a black box. Although one would not know what organizational structure was in the box at any point in time, it would be sufficient for the kinds of questions economists usually ask to know that the most efficient structure was there. The existence or environmental slack allows for the appearance of organizational slack and makes interesting the question of how organizations evolve and cope with the problems transaction costs raise.

The literature on transaction costs efficiencies is the subject of a separate survey in this series by David Teece.[3] It is not the subject matter of the present essay. Rather, I take a more macro perspective of the corporation and its evolution. The focus is on the corporation as a single organism, on the size and growth of this organism. The focus is on the interaction of the corporation with its external environment, not upon its internal adjustment processes. I seek to explain the patterns of size, growth and diversification that emerge over time.

B. The birth of firms

Schumpeter described the innovator–entrepreneur as one who

> First of all, [has] the dream and the will to found a private kingdom, usually, though not necessarily, also a dynasty. The modern world really does not know any such positions, but what may be attained by industrial or commercial success is still the nearest approach to medieval lordship possible to modern man. Its fascination is specially strong for people who have no other chance of achieving social distinction. The sensation of power and independence loses nothing by the fact that both are largely illusions. Closer analysis would lead to discovering an endless variety within this group of motives, from spiritual ambition down to mere snobbery. But this need not detain us. Let it suffice to point out that motives of this kind, although they stand nearest to consumers' satisfaction, do not coincide with it.
>
> Then there is the will to conquer: the impulse to fight, to prove oneself superior to others, to succeed for the sake, not of the fruits of success, but of success itself. From this aspect, economic action becomes akin to sport—there are financial races, or rather boxing-matches. The financial result is a secondary consideration, or, at all events, mainly valued as an index of success and as a symptom of victory, the displaying of which very often is more important as a motive of large expenditure than the wish for the consumers' goods themselves. Again we should find countless nuances, some of which, like social ambition, shade into the first group of motives. And again we are faced with a motive characteristically different from that of "satisfaction of wants" in the sense defined above, or from, to put the same thing into other words, "hedonistic adaptation."

---

[3] See David Teece's monograph in this series, "Theory of the Firm and Internal Organization."

Finally, there is the joy of creating, of getting things done, or simply of exercising one's energy and ingenuity. This is akin to a ubiquitous motive, but nowhere else does it stand out as an independent factor of behavior with anything like the clearness with which it obtrudes itself in our case. Our type seeks out difficulties, changes in order to change, delights in ventures. This group of motives is the most distinctly anti-hedonist of the three. (Schumpeter, 1934, pp. 93–4).

In the Schumpeterian schema, it is the innovator–entrepreneur who disturbs the economy's circular flow equilibrium, an equilibrium in which money flows from consumer to producer to factor owner, providing a normal return to the latter. It is he who causes economic development, ". . . a distinct phenomenon, entirely foreign to what may be observed in the circular flow or in the tendency towards equilibrium. It is spontaneous and discontinuous change in the channels of the flow, disturbance of the equilibrium, which forever alters and displaces the equilibium state previously existing" (1934, p. 64). Development occurs through the introduction of "new combinations" of product characteristics, production techniques, marketing methods, sources of supply, and organizational forms, i.e. through the introduction of innovations. Innovations lift the economy out of its circular flow equilibrium, innovations are the source of development. Profits are the rewards to the iconoclastic entrepreneur, who brings about economic development.

While in principle these iconoclastic-entrepreneurs could reside in a large, established firm, one's preconceptions of the behavioral selection biases of large organizations makes it seem unlikely. Indeed, Schumpeter's inconoclast–entrepreneur seems to have much the same personality traits as Anthony Downs's new bureau heads, "zealots who have a specific idea they want to put into practice on a large scale" (1967, p. 5). Zealots and iconoclasts seem more likely to be at home in a small new firm. So it appears Schumpeter also believed, at least as late as 1934. "[N]ew combinations are, as a rule, embodied, as it were, in new firms which generally do not arise out of the old ones but start producing beside them; . . . in general, it is not the owner of stage coaches who builds railways" (1934, p. 66). The semiconductor industry provides a more up-to-date illustration of Schumpeter's view. In 1953, a writer in *Fortune,* obviously either unaware of or unimpressed by Schumpeter's argument, would assert, "In a couple of years, when production figures take on more meaning, no one should be surprised if the leading transistor makers turn out to be today's leading tube makers: R.C.A., G.E., Ratheon, Sylvania" (Bello, 1953, p. 129). But, to Mr. Bello's apparent surprise, it would be Texas Instruments, a small geophysical services company prior to entering the semiconductor industry, which would develop the commercial applications of semiconductor technology furthest, and emerge as dominant firm in the industry, with other outsiders like Fairchild also capturing large market shares.

Of course, it was in AT&T's Bell Laboratories that the transistor was first invented. But, this case is certainly the exception that proves the rule. Protected from market competition by regulation until very recently, AT&T could afford to allow Bell Laboratories to create a research environment far more like that of a university than that of a corporate laboratory. It was in this unique research environment that John Bardeen, W. H. Brattain, and William Shockley were to conduct the basic research on semiconductors that was to lead to the transistor's invention and to earn them a Nobel prize.[4] The highly uncertain, basic research conducted on semiconductors at Bell labs after World War II bears little resemblance to the low-risk R&D on minor innovations which goes on in most corporate laboratories.[5]

Schumpeter does not indicate why innovations are to be expected from newcomers rather than established firms, but more modern treatments of the subject provide at least three explanations. First, the established firm may already be earning a profit (rent) in the industry. The profits to the stagecoach manufacturer from successfully introducing the railroad are the above normal returns from the railroad *less* the rents on its stagecoach business, wiped out by the railroad (Arrow, 1961; Kamien and Schwartz, 1982, ch. 4). The greater the rents on the existing line of business, the smaller the incentive to develop an innovation that will destroy

---

[4] For an excellent account of the transistor's invention, see Richard R. Nelson (1961).

[5] On the latter, see Mansfield, *et al.* (1971, ch. 2), and Mansfield, *et al.* (1977, ch. 2).

them. For the newcomer, gross and net profit from an innovation are one and the same.[6]

Second, the small firm does not experience the control loss and information distortion problems of the large, rigidly structured company (Monsen and Downs, 1965; Williamson, 1967, 1970, ch. 2). These problems are likely to be particularly important with respect to important innovations (Williamson, 1970, pp. 157–60, Normann, 1971). Radical departures appear to emerge most readily out of flexible organizational structures (Abernathy, 1978, p. 71 ff.), out of the kind of open, informal, high trust environments that are more readily established in the small firm (Klein, 1977, pp. 161–75).

Third, the small firm provides better incentives to management to undertake the tremendous risks surrounding major innovations. When Haloid's top management decided to "bet their company" on the xerography invention, they put up their own savings as well as the time and energy needed to see the development through. The success of the innovation made them, now the top managers of newly-named Xerox, into multimillionaires, whose pictures were commonly featured in the leading business magazines and news-

---

[6] A good example of how the existence of even modest rents can deter incumbent firms from innovating (or imitating) is the U.K. dry cleaning industry after World War II (Shaw, 1973).

Not only can existing rents be a deterrent to innovation, pending losses may be a stimulant to it. In the late '40s, the Haloid Company was a small photopaper manufacturer sharing both the city of Rochester and the photopaper market with Eastman Kodak. Haloid's profits were miniscule and its future existence in question, its management was casting about for new ideas and ventures to save the company. Its Vice President of Research and Development, John Dessauer, read about the photocopying process Chester Carlson had invented in a chemical engineering magazine, and took the initiative in obtaining patent licenses on what eventually became xerography. A Kodak or even an IBM, which did not at that time have a product that would be seriously challenged by xerography, were simply not unprofitable enough, not "hungry" enough, to take a chance on such a high risk innovation as xerography. Kodak and IBM were among some 20 large corporations, which Carlson approached with his innovation, that turned down the chance of licensing the patents.

In a similar vein, Carlson himself said he would never have invented xerography had he graduated from Cal Tech in the '50s or '60s, for he would then have been able to get a high paying job in an ongoing R&D laboratory and would have had little incentive to spend nights and weekends working on the invention as he did in the '30s. For Carlson, the necessity of making a living and supporting his invalid mother during the Depression proved to be the mother of invention. (Based on interviews with Carlson and Dessauer conducted by the author in the late '60s.)

papers (*Forbes,* 1965). No large corporation offers incentive packages to its middle-management that promise these kinds of rewards in exchange for taking the kinds of risks involved in the development of xerography. Perhaps this explains why creative R&D personnel in large firms who wish to pursue important, innovative ideas, typically leave the large firm to start their own company, as for example in transistors (Tilton, 1971, pp. 49–55).

These factors help to explain why the independent inventor, the university research team and other outsiders have remained a major source of important inventions.[7] Jewkes, Sawers and Stillerman's investigation of the origin of 61 important inventions attributed only 12 to large corporations (1969). Grosvenor (1929) attributed 12 of 72 major inventions between 1889 and 1929 to corporate laboratories and Hamberg (1963) listed large corporations as the source of major inventions in only 7 of the 27 cases he examined for the decade 1946–55.

Thus, the small or newly born firm is a primary source of new products and innovations, just as new products and innovations are the primary cause for the birth of new firms.[8] Few counter examples come to mind.[9] Rather, the typical large firm today is one which came into existence at the birth of a new product (Kodak) or if it entered a mature industry did so by introducing an important product or production process innovation (Polaroid).

C. The product life cycle

At the beginning of its evolution, the growth and development of a firm is closely entwined with growth and development of its main

---

[7] For surveys of this literature, see Hamberg (1966), Mueller and Tilton (1969), Kamien and Schwartz (1982, pp. 64–70), Scherer (1980, pp. 415–18).

[8] The innovations need not accompany the firm's founding. Haloid was a small, fifty year old company when it acquired the rights to the Carlson patent, which led to its rebirth as Xerox. Texas Instruments moved into transistors.

[9] As so often is the case, mergers can provide an exception to the rule. Litton Industries was started in 1953 by a group of managers, who left Ford to build a company via acquisitions. If innovation is involved in the growth of Litton, it would seem to be in the management's ability to finance one merger after another without the aid of other innovations, a feat successfully accomplished until the conglomerate merger bubble broke at the end of the sixties. The story of Litton's rise is recounted by Harris (1958), Rieser (1963), Seligman and Wise (1966), and *Business Week* (April 16, 1966). The decline is described in Rukeyser (1968), *Business Week* (Jan. 27, 1968), and *Forbes* (Feb. 15, 1968 and Dec. 1, 1969).

product(s). The hypothesis that products pass through a cycle in which the rate of growth of output first expands rapidly, but eventually declines, has been around for a long time. The classic study of product life cycles was by Arthur F. Burns in 1934. Burns studied the output histories of 147 products beginning as far back as 1870, and claimed to observe a general pattern of retardation in output growth rates for each product after some point in time. More recent investigations of 140 products by Polli and Cook (1969), and of 46 products by Gort and Klepper (1982) appear to confirm that products typically do pass through a common pattern of development, although with important exceptions and caveats to be noted. The salient features of this common pattern are as follows:

1) The rate of growth of output is rapid at first, and then declines. Burns observed continual declines in output growth rates for the products he examined, and the same is true on average for the Gort and Klepper sample. But Bela Gold (1964), in a follow-up study to Burns's, found undiminished rates of growth for many products over long time periods. No downward trend in output growth was apparent to me in 9 of the 46 products in the Gort and Klepper study over the latter segments of their reported data.[10] Thus, if one envisages a product's life cycle as an S-shaped curve with output on the vertical axis and time on the horizontal, then the segment of the curve at which its concavity reverses may be a straight line of considerable length (cf. Gold, 1964, p. 58).

2) The number of firms in the industry rises at first, then a "shakeout" occurs in which there is a rapid exit of sellers. This period is followed by a mature phase in which no systematic pattern of change in the number of firms in the industry is observed (Gort and Klepper, 1982; Klepper and Graddy, 1984).

3) Initial entrants are typically small and are often newly formed companies, including spinoffs from existing companies. (Gort and Klepper, 1982; Klepper and Graddy, 1984; Abernathy, 1978; Tilton, 1971). Entry is "know-how" determined and the critical human inputs are scientific and engineering (Hirsch, 1972).

---

[10] Electric shavers after 1935, jet propelled engines after 1951, fluorescent lamps after 1942, freezers after 1949, outboard motors after 1939, penicillin after 1949, phonograph records after 1918, tires after 1914, and zippers after 1926. See, Klepper and Graddy, 1984, Table 4.

4) The rate of technological change is at first rapid, but then slows. Early innovations tend to be focussed on product design changes, on improving quality rather than reducing costs. Many innovations at the early stages come from outside the industry, e.g. from universities or customers. As output grows and "dominant" product designs are hit upon, innovation is oriented more towards process improvements and cost reduction. Firms inside the industry begin to account for an increasing fraction of innovations.[11]

It is interesting that this process of product evolution appears equally applicable to recent innovations like transistors and xerography as to earlier innovations like automobiles and automobile tires. For it seems to resemble in many respects the process of economic development Joseph Schumpeter first described at the turn of the century.[12] Schumpeter stressed that each innovation brings with it a "crowd" of imitators (1934, p. 133), which corresponds well to the rapid growth in number of producers occurring during the early phases of a product's life cycle. The "shakeout" periods that inevitably come eliminating many early entrants might be equated to Schumpeter's "perrenial gale of creative destruction."

D. The emergence of dominant firms

The innovative-entrepreneur's task is to create a firm and in the case of a new product innovation to create an industry. If one takes a Knightian view toward profit and assumes that it is the reward for uncertainty bearing, then the innovator–entrepreneur can be thought of as a creator of uncertainty, disturbing market equilibria by introducing new products and processes, gambling on his ability to predict the future success of the innovations despite the uncertainty that shrouds that future (Mueller, 1976). The task of the management of the established firm is to preserve rents already extant, to preserve the first-mover advantages inherited from the

---

[11] Mansfield, *et al.* (1971, pp. 173–81). Abernathy (1978, ch. 4); Buzzell and Nourse (1966), Harvey (1968), Utterback (1979).

[12] Schumpeter's early description of economic development has also inspired Nelson and Winter's recent evolutionary theory (1982).

For a recent attempt to model the Schumpeterian process rigorously, see Reinganum (1985).

founding entrepreneur. It must control uncertainty if not eliminate it (Klein, 1977, pp. 12–24). Thus, as the corporation passes from young, small innovator in an uncertain, dynamic market to mature market leader in a stable growing market, profit creating needs give way to rent preserving strategies (Klein, 1977, ch. 5).

As an industry matures, competition within the industry shifts from an emphasis on product quality and product improvements to an emphasis on price (Hirsch, 1972). Product design innovations are displaced by process innovations. Major innovations give way to minor ones. Dynamic goals of improving product quality or production techniques are replaced by the static goals of meeting production quotas, maintaining quality control and cost control. Management becomes the critical human input (Hirsch, 1972). Here cause and effect cannot be separated. The maturing successful firm experiences greater bureaucratization, slower change in product design, and greater standardization and specificity in production technique, and the one cannot easily be separated from the other.[13]

Many of these changes are the inevitable accompaniments of size. The small firm is almost by definition decentralized. It can maintain the flat, fluid informal organizational structure that is required to cope with rapid technological change. It can maintain the high trust, personal relationships that are essential to sustain organizational stability in an uncertain environment (Klein, 1977, chs. 5, 6). As the company grows larger, increases in formality and hierarchy become almost inevitable (Klein, 1977, chs. 5, 6; Williamson, 1975, chs. 3, 7; Abernathy, 1978, ch. 4). With these changes in organizational structure come not surprisingly changes in management "style." Schumpeter's iconoclastic entrepreneur and Downs's zealot are replaced by managers better suited to the formal hierarchical structure now in place, managers, who both lay down the rules and enforce and preserve them, managers Downs describes as "conservers" (1966, p. 19).

Growth in size typically brings with it another important change in the structure of the firm. The demand for investment funds for the truly successful growing firm outstrip the supply of capital that can be generated internally. The founding entrepreneur-capitalist

---

[13] Harvey (1968), Klein (1977), Abernathy (1978), Gort and Klepper (1982), Klepper and Graddy (1984).

ownership interests in the firm must be diluted (Marris, 1964, pp. 5–11). Thus, growth in size brings with it both an increase in formality and bureaucratization that separates the leadership of the firm from the firm, and a dilution of the financial interests of the leadership driving a wedge between management interests and those of pure ownership.

The time required for an industry's life cycle to enfold can vary considerably. When it enfolds slowly, the entrepreneurial founder retires before major overhauls in the firm's organizational structure are required, and the management changes can be effected smoothly through the appropriate selection of second and third generation management. But, occasionally a company's development proceeds so rapidly, or errors are made in selecting new managers, so that the company finds itself in the maturing cost control phase of its development, with an informal control structure and entrepreneurial leader.

A good example of this is the firm E. J. Korvette. Korvette was the first of the discount department stores. It was founded by Eugene Ferkauf shortly after World War II. Ferkauf was a classic entrepreneurial type: imaginative, hard working, a risk-taker, slightly eccentric in his personal habits. The innovative idea behind the discount store was fairly simple. Sell popular items at low prices, by maintaining low profit margins. This pricing policy was to be accomplished by stocking only the most popular brands and models of each item, not offering the same level of services as traditional retailers (no charge accounts, no time credit plans, no free delivery, fewer sales personnel) and less luxurious, indeed often warehouse-like, stores. Obviously, for a low-price, low margin sales strategy to succeed, controlling costs and maintaining sales volume were essential. Ferkauf made sure these goals were met in the early years by personally going from store to store to supervise operations. Indeed, he had no office of his own.

Success led to growth and Ferkauf pushed Korvette's expansion in three directions: adding new outlets within its base New York area market; geographic expansion up and down the Eastern seaboard and into the Midwest; the addition of new selling lines like food and furniture. Some "frill services" like charge plans were also added. During the height of the shakeout period from August, 1961, to the end of 1965, Korvette's floor space more than tripled and the number of its department stores increased from 11 to 39. Ferkauf's informal, personal management style proved inadequate to the enhanced managerial challenge. Earnings per share began to decline in 1965. Korvette was acquired by Spartan Industries in August of 1966.

Thus, to survive the shakeout period, a company's founders must do more than just select the right product designs and production techniques and keep pace with the rapid changes of the early phases of the product life cycle. To develop into a mature industry leader a firm must be able to adopt the changes in organizational structure and style that will allow it to grow with its market. If the entrepreneurial founders are not of a temperament or age to steer the firm through this phase of growth, new leadership will be required, managers capable of preserving and consolidating the firm's position as market leader, organizers and conservers with attenuated financial interests in the firm. It is these professional managers that one finds at the helm when the corporation enters its third evolutionary phase, that of the mature industry leader.

Part II

MANAGERIAL CAPITALISM

E. Maturity: stable internal growth, external growth and decline

Firms are born, grow, and in cases like E. J. Korvette die. This cycle of development has suggested to several observers the analogy between the firm and other living organisms.

> We may read a lesson from the young trees of the forest as they struggle upwards through the benumbing shade of their older rivals. Many succumb on the way, and a few only survive; those few become stronger with every year, they get a larger share of light and air with every increase of their height, and at last in their turn they tower above their neighbours, and seem as though they would grow on for ever, and for ever become stronger as they grow. But they do not. One tree will last longer in full vigour and attain a greater size than another; but sooner or later age tells on them all. Though the taller ones have a better access to light and air than their rivals, they gradually lose vitality; and one after another they give place to others, which, though of less material strength, have on their side the vigour of youth.
>
> And with the growth of trees, so was it with the growth of businesses as a general rule before the great recent development of vast joint-stock companies, which often stagnate, but do not readily die (Marshall, 1920, p. 263).

While Alfred Marshall clearly thought that an analogy could be drawn between that manmade organization the firm and biological organisms, he also thought there was a difference at least since the advent of the joint-stock company. Trees, like men, must die, but the modern corporation can survive indefinitely. Maturation and immortality can coexist in the large firm, a fact of considerable importance in understanding the evolution of modern capitalism.

But while the development of the joint-stock company could confer immortality on the firm, Marshall seemed to agree with Adam Smith that this institutional innovation did not necessarily

21

lead to greater efficiency. The larger corporation could survive, but in a state of stagnation.

The implication would be that the firm's returns will decline as the corporation matures and "stagnates." John Hiller (1977) has undertaken one of the few direct studies of firm life-cycle effects on company returns. He traced a sample of 144 of the 200 largest U.S. corporations of 1973 back as far as 1929 and measured both average and marginal returns on capital. He found a continual decline in the *marginal* returns on capital of both young and mature firms over the post-World War II period, but the marginal returns of young firms remained substantially above those of mature companies throughout the period. Interesting also was the finding that average returns on capital, including monopoly rents, remained high for the mature firms in markets with very high entry barriers and were actually higher than those of young firms in these markets at the end of the period (see Table V). Thus, while aging brings with it declining marginal returns, mature firms with protected market positions can maintain high rents on capital over long periods. Hiller's results are consistent with those of other writers concerning the persistence of above normal returns (Qualls, 1974; Mueller, 1977a, 1986).

Several studies have examined the stability of market positions. They all reach the same conclusion. There is a definite regression on the mean effect. Firms with initial market shares substantially above

TABLE V
Marginal and average returns on capital for young and mature firms 1945–71

Firm Age	Barriers to entry	Returns	Years					
			1945	1950	1955	1960	1965	1971
Young	Very High	Marginal	77.6	63.9	54.1	36.2	23.0	14.1
	Substantial/Low	Marginal	56.7	44.2	59.2	48.2	20.5	16.5
	Very High	Average	—	69.7	98.2	81.8	75.9	43.2
	Substantial/Low	Average	—	33.7	65.8	83.7	85.9	56.5
Mature	Very High	Marginal	52.6	39.5	28.5	30.7	18.0	9.8
	Substantial/Low	Marginal	54.0	35.5	23.2	23.1	14.5	7.9
	Very High	Average	78.5	71.2	59.4	52.4	67.2	53.5
	Substantial/Low	Average	34.7	52.3	60.0	45.3	51.6	38.8

Source: Hiller (1977).
Notes: Sample size = 144.
All calculations based on an assumed 10% depreciation rate.

the average tend to lose market share over time. But the market share erosion process works slowly and in many markets does not work at all. Counteracting it are the first-mover advantages incumbents have with buyers (Schmalensee, 1982), and the learning-by-doing cost advantages of incumbents (Arrow, 1962; Rosen, 1972; Spence, 1981; Smiley and Ravid, 1983). Many companies are the leading sellers in their markets from one decade to the next. Thus, although several of the 18 companies Shepherd examined with 1948 market shares of 50 percent or more experienced substantial declines in their market shares by 1973 (e.g. Du Pont's cellophane went from 90 percent to 60 percent), 15 of the 18 still had market shares of 50 percent or more in 1973.[14] Similarly, Weiss and Pascoe (1983) found that 18 of the 23 companies with 1950 market shares of 40 percent or more in their sample, continued to have market shares above 40 percent in 1975.

I examined 350 *roughly* comparable markets in 1950 and 1972. I found that in 142 of the 350 markets the same company was the leading firm in both 1950 and 1972, and in another 13 the same two firms were industry leaders but with reversed ranks in the two years (Mueller, 1986, Table III). Dominant firms do not always decline.[15]

Substantial evidence also exists indicating that market leadership brings with it above normal returns. A strong positive correlation exists between profitability and market share[16] Those firms which have succeeded in obtaining a large market share can earn persistently above normal returns if they retain it. Their rate of growth will be equal to that of their industry and thus may gradually decline over time as the industry's products are displaced. But a leading firm may continue to enjoy an above normal return and a

---

[14] Shepherd (1975, p. 309, Table B.2). A great attrition of market positions is apparent between 1910 and 1935 (see, p. 308, Table B.1), but Shepherd is surely correct in his conjecture that the market shares of 1910 were artificially high having been brought about by the great trust-creating merger wave in the preceding two decades. In 1948, by way of contrast, there had been no appreciable merger activity for 19 years.

[15] The hypothesis that dominant firms do decline has as its intellectual antecedent the classic paper by Worcester (1957) and as its factual bellwether United States Steel Corporation. For a critical reappraisal, see Geroski (1985).

[16] See, Imel and Helmberger, 1971; Gale, 1972; Shepherd, 1972, 1975; Gale and Branch, 1982; Ravenscraft, 1983; Smirlock, Gilligan, and Marshall, 1984; and Mueller, 1985b.

modest growth rate for decade after decade. Some firms have been content to do just that.

A good example is Maytag. In 1950 it was the second leading seller of laundry equipment in the United States with a market share of 0.143 and a return on capital 96 percent above the average large manufacturing firm. In the early seventies, its sales were still concentrated in laundry equipment and it remained a leader in this market. Its long run projected return on assets was more than three times the projected return of the average company. In 1982, Peters and Waterman would include Maytag in their sample of best-managed companies based on its overall performance from 1960 through 1980. Another student of business singled Maytag out as having a successful "survival strategy" in the hostile environment of the seventies (Forbes, 1970). It would appear that Maytag is likely to survive and prosper so long as washing and drying machines are sold in the United States.

Despite its survival record and enviable profit performance, Maytag has never been one of the 100 largest United States manufacturing corporations, nor will it ever become one so long as it continues to specialize in laundry equipment. If Maytag's management wanted to join the exclusive, 100 largest club, Maytag would have to diversify. The same inference can be drawn from the relatively low marginal rates of return for mature companies Hiller (1977) estimated. Further, internal expansion by additional investment in a mature company's base industry promises below normal profits and growth.

A company can expand more rapidly than its product market without leaving it by increasing its market share. To do so by internal growth means the displacement of existing sellers, with all of the hostile oligopolistic responses one expects from this type of strategy. Thus, those companies which seek to grow more rapidly than their markets are growing, but do not wish to diversify, can be expected to engage in horizontal acquisitions.

Until the Celler–Kefauver Amendment closed the door in 1950 on horizontal acquisitions of any appreciable magnitude, this form of merger was dominant in the United States.[17] Horizontal mergers remain dominant in Europe (Hughes and Singh, 1980). These facts

---

[17] Stigler (1950), Markham (1955), Nelson (1959), Reid (1968), and Eis (1969).

should be kept in mind. With the rise in the importance of diversification mergers in the United States since 1950, a plethora of hypotheses have appeared describing the various efficiencies, synergies or market power advantages these mergers produce.[18] Yet it would appear that U.S. firms would have eschewed the newly discovered efficiency advantages of diversification acquisitions post-1950, as European corporations did by-and-large, had U.S. antitrust policy allowed them to do so. The return to horizontal mergers by steel and petroleum firms in the United States under the more lax antimerger policies of the Reagan administration further confirms this point.

There exists an obvious upper bound to expansion within a market. Moreover, as market concentration levels grow high, even permissive antitrust policies begin to deter expansion by horizontal merger. Thus, we find the need to shift toward diversification to further growth appearing in Europe in recent years, as it precipitiously arose in the United States in 1950.[19]

With diversification comes the need for further organizational change. While the organizational structure remains essentially hierarchical, the addition of several new products or product lines essentially adds several, parallel hierarchical pyramids to the firm. The consequence is most usually that the traditional, hierarchical pyramid, what Williamson calls the U-form organization is replaced by an M-form structure.[20] In the M-form, separate product lines or geographic areas become divisions and a central management team handles long range planning, raising capital and its allocation across divisions, and other similar common requirements of the diversified firm's portfolio of products.

The M-form organization's top management is incapable of being expert in all of the product or geographic areas in which its firm operates and thus tends to be expert in none. M-form managers are

---

[18] See, Steiner (1975, chs. 2–6), Scherer (1980, pp. 127–41), and many of the papers in the *St. John's Law Review, Special Edition* on conglomerate mergers (Spring 1970).

[19] On Europe, see Hughes and Singh (1980), Channon (1973), Pavan (1972), Gorecki (1975), and Dyas and Thanheiser (1976); on the United States, Berry (1975) and Scherer and Ravenscraft (1984).

[20] For a comparison of the M- and U-forms and discussion of their relative merits, see Chandler (1962, 1977), Williamson (1970, 1975, 1979, 1981), Caves (1980), and Teece's forthcoming contribution to this series (ftn. 3).

typically generalists trained in finance, accounting and the law as befits the general services they supply to the firm, in contrast to the backgrounds in engineering, production and marketing that dominated in U-form firms.[21]

The theoretical and empirical literature on the M-form organization presents a convincing case for the proposition that the M-form organizational structure is generally superior to the U-form for companies with diversified product lines or geographically dispersed distribution or production operations. But this same literature typically does not address the question of whether the M-form diversified company is in aggregate more efficient than a group of autonomous companies producing the same set of products would be. That is, the M-form literature does not directly deal with the questions of whether there exist managerial diseconomies of scale, whether there exist limits to the size of the firm.

One of the pioneering investigations of the limits-to-the-size-of-firm question in the economics literature is by Oliver Williamson (1967). Williamson poses the question as basically one of efficiency in processing information. To exercise effective control of the organization, its leaders must gather information from the bottom layers and send down commands based on the information gathered. Williamson assumes, based on experiments in the organizational science literature, that information gets lost or its content distorted as it passes from one layer of the hierarchy to the next. He makes the crucial assumption that information loss in a hierarchical organization is cumulative, i.e. if α fraction of the information gathered at one level gets effectively transmitted to the next $(0 \leq \alpha \leq 1)$, then there is a cumulative loss of information in an organization of $n + 1$ hierarchical layers equal to $(1 - \alpha^n)$th of the information to be transferred. The assumption that information loss is cumulative in this way leads to the result that there is a determinate, optimal size of the firm, i.e. a size beyond which further expansion lowers both efficiency and profits.

Williamson views the information processing problem in an organization as one of passing information from one layer to the next all of the way from the bottom to top, and top to bottom. The

---

[21] On the differing backgrounds of chief executives, see Beam (1979), and Sussman (1979).

discovery of an R and D worker must *in effect* be transferred to the president for a decision to be made on it. The president's commands must work their way down to the R and D bench worker and lowest paid blue collar worker. This view of information passing all of the way through the organization, leads Williamson to cite examples of information distortion as messages from one person to another, of distortions in duplicating a picture as it passes from one person to another across a group of individuals.

But the control problem can be viewed differently. Calvo and Wellisz (1978), for example, view the *control* problem in a hierarchical organization as essentially a monitoring problem. At any level in the hierarchy an employee may exert less than the maximum possible effort, because he knows his efforts are only imperfectly monitored by his superior, i.e. there is only a fixed probability of being caught shirking. While shirking leads to a certain control loss or effort loss in the Calvo–Wellisz model, it is not cumulative. If the company's chosen probability of catching a given worker shirking leads him to exert α of his maximum potential effort, and the preferences and incentives at all levels in the hierarchy are the same, then the cumulative control loss in the firm in the Calvo–Welisz model is $1 - \alpha$. Each individual works $1 - \alpha$ less than his maximum potential effort and thus all work $1 - \alpha$ less, and the cumulative loss is only $1 - \alpha$ of the maximum potential output. Given the other assumptions of the Williamson and Calvo–Wellisz models, the result implies that there is no optimal limit to firm size.[22]

While information in the Williamson model must pass through all levels in the hierarchy, in the Calvo–Wellisz model it passes only from one level to the next highest level. A supervisor recognizes if his supervisee is shirking or not simply by observing the supervisee. If the supervisee is in turn a supervisor of a yet lower level in the hierarchy, it is not necessary under Calvo–Wellisz assumptions to also observe the still lower level employees to monitor the employees immediately beneath oneself in the hierarchy. If this

---

[22] The result also depends upon the assumption that each worker is ignorant of the times in which he/she will be monitored. Thus, each worker adjusts his/her effort to an optimal level given a probability of being monitored. If the workers can adjust effort with the knowledge of precisely when they will be monitored, a finite limit to firm size reemerges (Calvo and Wellisz, 1978, pp. 949–52).

assumption about the control problem in a hierarchical organization is more valid than Williamson's, then there are no effective limits to corporate size.[23]

Alternatively, both views of the control problem may be valid simultaneously. The modern corporation must process an immense variety of information. Some of it, like information on shirking, may only have to pass through one or a few layers of hierarchy. Efficiency may be preserved by the unanticipated monitoring of subordinate effort. Other pieces of information, characteristics of a radical, potentially important invention may have to go from one end of the organization to the other. If this view is accurate, there may exist finite limits to a company's ability to expand and process some kinds of information efficiently, but not with respect to other kinds of information.

The latter possibility becomes more plausible when one relaxes the assumption, implicit in all of the above models, that the "technology" of processing information is independent of firm size. Scale economies may well exist in information gathering and processing. A good example of such a scale economy is the scanners recently introduced in supermarkets in the U.S.A. Instead of reading every price, checkout personnel can now simply move the food item across a scanner and the price is recorded on the customer's checkout list by a computer. This invention improves the productivity of both the checkout worker and his or her supervisor; the computer can also keep track of how many food items per hour a given checkout worker has handled. Such computerized checkout systems are only economically justified for supermarket chains above some given size, however. Information handling technologies of this type raise still further the limits to firm size.

Intuitively, it would seem that the control loss problem is least serious or can be most readily circumvented technologically in static, unchanging environments. If the main managerial task is

---

[23] Camacho and White (1981) point out that under the assumptions of the Calvo–Wellisz model (all workers of like tastes and abilities, and essentially constant returns to scale), there will never be any firms of size greater than one employee. A larger firm produces only α $(0 < \alpha < 1)$ of what the N individuals who make up that firm could produce themselves. Thus, each individual will choose to be self-employed.

For a different derivation of the no-limit-to-size-result, see Mirrlees (1976).

policing shirking, and demand and cost conditions, product quality, etc., are unchanging, information gathering can be routinized to a considerable degree. But in a rapidly changing environment, or in areas in which change is inherent in the task, as in the introduction of innovations, the relevant information to be gathered and the criteria for monitoring performance are so varied that information and control loss problems must loom large.[24]

Ironically, perhaps, these considerations suggest that the diversified M-form firm should fair best when its portfolio of products does not include markets in which uncertainty plays a large role or technological change is most rapid. Not being expert on its individual product lines, the M-form's top management team relies on general indicators of performance from its divisions: return on capital, price-cost margin, growth in sales or profits. These indicators of performance may be reliable in the short run, when the firm's market environment is unchanging. But when its environment is in flux or in the long run when change and innovation may be necessary, these general indicators of performance often prove to be inadequate. The classic "control problem" in an M-form firm is the discovery that a division that appeared to be doing very well yesterday is in deep trouble today.[25]

But the issue cannot be fully settled theoretically. The M-form organization allows for some increased decentralization and that could work to make this type of firm more innovative. In the end one must examine the evidence, which we shall now do.

F. Diversification: Size, growth and profitability

The need to diversify to increase size and sustain growth is virtually a logical necessity when viewed in the context of the firm's life cycle. Both Edith Penrose (1959, pp. 144–45, 212–14) and Robin Marris (1964, pp. 60–1, 119–22) have emphasized the essential role diversification plays in the long run growth of the firm. One need not be surprised, therefore, to learn that size and diversification have been consistently found to be positively correlated, as have

---

[24] Williamson notes that large corporations may have difficulties coming up with important innovations (1975, pp. 184–87).

[25] A classic example is General Dynamics' problems with its Convair division in the early 1960s (Smith, 1966, chs. 3, 4). Evans Products ran into similar control problems with its railroad car division somewhat later (McDonald, 1967).

changes in diversification and growth.[26] Were the results any different, one would question the data or statistical techniques. Let us move on to issues more in doubt.

The first is the link between diversification and profitability. Several writers have presented hypotheses describing certain situations in which diversification could increase profitability. Stanley Boyle (1972) and Stephen Rhoades (1973) have argued that diversification by firms with above normal profits conceals the magnitude of these profits from potential entrants, thus raising entry barriers. These enhanced entry barriers allow the diversified companies to maintain or enhance their profits in their base markets.

Weston (1970) and Williamson (1970) have emphasized the advantages of the M-form organization as a mini-capital market internal to the firm.[27] When profitable investment opportunities arise in some divisions, central management can supply these divisions with capital, drawing from other parts of the firm with less attractive investment opportunities or rely on its size and the scope of its operations to raise capital cheaply in the external capital market. A division with an investment opportunity of great potential can raise capital within the diversified firm without the parent unit's losing possession of the information about the investment opportunity.[28] With appropriability of information problems mitigated, more investment in information gathering (e.g. R&D) can take place. Moreover, the transmission of capital from low to high marginal return areas within the firm can be "fine-tuned" to a degree to which the external capital market is incapable.

---

[26] See studies of the United States by Gort (1962) and Berry (1975), of Canada by Caves, et al. (1980), and of the United Kingdom by Hassid (1975, 1977).

[27] The Weston–Williamson hypothesis involves the advantages of M-form organizational forms and not just diversification, but diversification is a necessary condition for achieving these efficiencies. Moreover, the distinction between a multidivisional company and a diversified company is today all but meaningless. Wrigley (1970) found that 80 percent of the Fortune 500 of 1970 were diversified and 86 percent had a multidivisional organizational form. Given that a substantial fraction of the 14 percent, which were not M-forms were single product or dominant product firms, the overlap is obviously considerable.

[28] Note the similarity between the Boyle–Rhoades hypothesis and those of Weston and Williamson. Both hinge in part on the successful concealment of profit rate information by diversification, although one set of authors views this as enhancing market power, the other as enhancing efficiency.

More recently, Baumol, Panzer, and Willig (1982) have added elegance and generality to the diversification–profitability hypothesis, through the development of the "economies of scope" concept. If one presumes that managers always seek to maximize profits, and that economies of scope are present, then diversified firms should be more profitable.

Empirical evidence on the relationship between profitability and diversification is mixed and difficult to interpret. A positive correlation between profitability and diversification has been found by Rhoades (1973) and Carter (1977). Lecraw (1984) found a positive correlation between profits and diversification among Canadian companies but only when they were diversified into related businesses.[29] Lecraw's finding for Canada was corroborated in a follow-up study by Rhoades (1974) to his earlier work. While in 1973 Rhoades published a paper indicating that diversification outside of one's major 4-digit industry is positively related to profitability, Rhoades' 1974 study measured diversification in a broader fashion, i.e. as diversification out of the firm's major $2\frac{1}{2}$ to 3 digit product area. This more broadly measured degree of diversification was *negatively* related to profitability. I also found a negative relationship, once I controlled for the predicted profits of a firm based on its market share and product differentiation (1986, ch. 7). Miller (1969) found no relationship between profitability and diversification whatsoever.

Particularly difficult to disentangle in these studies is the direction of causality. If diversification takes place to conceal above normal returns, then diversifying companies have above normal profits in their base industries prior to any diversification activity they undertake. Similarly, if diversification is motivated by a pure desire to grow larger even without any increase in profitability, the R and D or mergers that lead to diversification must somehow be financed. Those firms earning above normal returns in their basic product lines are in a better position to finance unprofitable diversification. If the diversification activity does not entirely wipe out the above normal returns precipitating it, then profits and diversification will again be positively correlated. To test whether diversification *caused*

---

[29] Lecraw's result here may be related to John Scott's (1982) finding that multi-market contact and profitability are positively related. Scott's results imply that very specific kinds of diversification *when jointly undertaken* can be profitable.

higher profits one would have to measure profits both before and after diversification, not simply correlate *ex post* levels of each.

Several writers have remarked upon the causality issue. Berry regressed the increase in diversification between 1960–65 on 1960 earnings, and found generally positive coefficients, although they were only statistically significant when diversification was into 4-digit industries in the same 2-digit industries in which the diversifying firm operated (1975, pp. 120–105). Note the similarity between Berry's findings and those of Lecraw (1984) and Rhoades, but with the causality inference reversed.

Jesse Markham confronted the causality issue in his investigation of diversification, and his observations warrant repeating:

> In almost all models in which profitability and price-earnings ratios entered as statistically significant, they took on a negative sign. This inverse relationship between profitability and both 1970 company diversification and the volume of 1961–1970 diversifying acquisitions is consistent with any one of several hypotheses: It may . . . indicate that acquisitive conglomerates sacrifice profitability for growth; it may mean that companies earning relatively low rates of return in their present industries are the most active acquirers of companies in other industries; or, alternatively, it may simply mean that diversification through acquisition in 1961–70 was not generally an especially profitable activity.[30]

Thus, while growth and diversification are clearly positively related, the relationship between diversification and profitability is ambiguous both with respect to sign and causal interpretation.

Given that firm size and diversification are positively correlated, one might expect to find the same ambiguous relationship between firm size and profitability as exists between diversification and profitability. But, the correlation between size and diversification is not so strong as to make the relationship between profitability and size a foregone conclusion. A brief look at this literature is therefore warranted.

Early studies by Crum (1939), Stekler (1963) and Stigler (1963) reached the conclusion that above some rather minimal size,

---

[30] Markham (1973, p. 160) cites Gilbert (1971) in further support of the multiple interpretation to the profitability-diversification correlation.

profitability and size are unrelated. Given that a greater fraction of economic profits are likely to appear as costs in small firms where owners and managers are more often one and the same (Stigler, 1963, pp. 59–61), these early findings seemed to refute the notion that big firms are able to earn higher profits.

Hall and Weiss (1967) selected a sample of companies they believed to be sufficiently large to be above minimum efficient scale and found a positive correlation between profitability and the log of assets (more accurately a negative correlation between profitability and one over the log of assets), after controlling for other variables. Their paper has become the standard reference for the conclusion that profits and absolute size are positively related. But the Hall and Weiss findings were soon challenged by Marcus (1969), and Weiss himself has expressed some doubt concerning the result in personal communication with the writer, since he has not been able to reproduce the original findings. Bradley Gale (1972) did get positive coefficients on firm size in all six of the equations he estimated, but the variable was significant in only two. While generally taking on a positive sign in my work, it also was typically insignificant (1986, chs. 6 and 7).

Outside of the United States all observers have found either no relationship between profitability and size or a negative one. Singh and Whittington (1968) found no significant differences in the average profitability of UK firms across different size classes. Samuels and Smyth (1968) found a negative relationship between profitability and size for quoted UK companies. In France, studies by Morvan (1972) and Jenny and Weber (1976) both find profitability and firm size to be negatively related. Jacquemin and Saëz (1976) found a negative relationship between size and profitability within a sample of large European and Japanese companies (see also Jacquemin and Cardon, 1973). Outside of the United States, there is no evidence whatsoever that, beyond the smallest size class, bigger firms earn higher profits. Within the United States, the evidence is ambiguous.

No company management chooses to diversify without weighing the consequences of the decision. Firms need not diversify and grow so large that they become members of the top 500, or 200, or 100. If size and diversification do not bring with them increases in profitability, and perhaps even declines, the questions arise: Why do managers choose to expand and diversify when they could remain small, or more accurately, medium sized? What are the implications of nonprofitable corporate expansion for the allocation of capital in society and the overall efficiency of the economy?

A frequently discussed motivation for diversification is to reduce the variability in a firm's profitability.[31] When profit streams **a** and **b** are combined in proportions α and $1 - \alpha$, then the variance on the combined portfolio is

$$\sigma_c^2 = \alpha^2 \sigma_a^2 + \alpha(1 - \alpha)r_{ab}\sigma_a\sigma_b + (1 - \alpha)^2\sigma_b^2$$

where r_{ab} is the correlation between the **a** and **b** profit streams. When the two profit streams are not perfectly correlated ($r_{ab} < 1$), the variance of the combined profit stream is less than the simple weighted sum of the variances on the two separate streams. The return on **c**, R_c is equal to the weighted sum of the two returns, however

$$R_c = \alpha R_a + (1 - \alpha)R_b$$

Thus, risk (variance) is reduced by diversification for a given level of return. The preponderance of empirical evidence confirms that size and diversification are negatively related to profit variability.[32] But it is also now well-established that shareholders can achieve superior diversification in their holdings of shares than it is possible for firms to achieve through diversification of real assets.[33] If management seeks to maximize ownership's welfare, then diversification which does not increase the returns on the combined activities is not a defensible strategy.

Reduction in the variability of a firm's profits may be in the

---

[31] See discussions in Scherer (1980, pp. 104–08) and Jacquemin and deJonk (1977, pp. 90–94, 114–17).

[32] Prais (1981, p. 97) discusses why the relationship should hold and shows size and profit variability to be negatively related in a hyperbolic fashion using data for the United States from Stekler (1964) and for the United Kingdom from Whittington (1971). See also for the United States, Winn (1977); for the United Kingdom, Singh and Whittington (1968), Samuels and Smyth (1968); for France, Morvan (1972); and for large European and Japanese firms (Jacquemin and Saëz (1976)). An exception to this general finding is Smyth, Boyes and Pessaw (1975).

[33] See Levy and Sarnat (1970), Smith (1970), and Azzi (1978).

The recent work of Roll (1977) and Levy (1983) demonstrates that the optimally diversified portfolio should contain *negative* positions in some shares. No firm can make negative investments in real assets.

management's interests. If the probability of a management's dismissal rises in a period of relatively low profitability, then smoothing profits over time even with some sacrifice in mean returns may reduce managerial risks.[34] Moreover, managers qua owners may not be able to trade away their shares in their companies to achieve diversified portfolios of shares, management's ability to protect itself from dismissal is directly related to its own shareholding (Mueller, 1986, ch. 7). Thus, while diversification may be an inefficient way to reduce the risks of outside owners, it may be attractive to managers whose wealth and income are heavily dependent on their company.

The other managerial motive for diversification is to avoid slow or declining growth prospects facing a firm in the mature phases of its life cycle. Weston and Mansinghka (1971) show that the companies that engaged in the most intensive conglomerate merger activity in the sixties had lower than average profit rates in the late fifties. They thus describe the merger strategies of these companies as "defensive diversification." While this motive for diversification is aptly named "defensive diversification," it is really separate from the risk reduction motive just discussed. The management of a company in a mature or declining industry knows with near certainty that its company is destined to stagnate and decline if it does not diversify. Diversification in this situation is to avoid the inevitable not to protect against the unknown. The question raised by the literature on profitability, size and diversification is whether this diversification activity serves any social purpose beyond preventing the decline of certain firms.

G. Returns on investment and the theory of the firm

If growth and diversification by mature companies do not increase their profitability, then the returns on investment of these firms should be below the opportunity cost of capital for their owners. Further evidence on the efficiency consequences of corporate growth and diversification can be found in estimates of the returns on investment for large, mature companies.

---

[34] See Caves and Yamey (1971) and with respect to diversifying mergers Amihud and Lev (1981).

What is at issue with respect to the efficiency of the allocation of capital are the *marginal* returns on investment. Thus, the many studies examining average returns on capital across firms and industries are, unfortunately, largely irrelevant to the question of whether on the margin mature firms invest optimally.

Several studies have appeared in recent years, however, which are relevant to the issue at hand. In a pioneering paper appearing in 1970, Baumol, Heim, Malkiel and Quandt (hereafter BHMQ) estimated the returns on investment out of ploughback and new debt and equity issues. Their methodology was as follows: Suppose today's profits are determined by today's capital stock, and both are presumed to persist indefinitely in the absence of further invest-ment. Let I dollars be invested today at a return of r. Then tomorrow's profits should exceed today's by rI. Letting $\Delta\pi_{t+1}$ stand for the change in profits between t and $t+1$, we have

$$\Delta\pi_{t+1} = rI_t$$

If the new investment earns r in perpetuity and I_{t+1} invested in period $t+1$ also earns r, then the increment in profits between t and $t+2$, $\Delta\pi_{t+2} = \pi_{t+2} - \pi_t$ should satisfy the relationship

$$\Delta\pi_{t+2} = r(I_t + I_{t+1})$$

Cumulating investment over k periods one has

$$\sum_{i=1}^{k} \Delta\pi_{t+1} = r \sum_{i=0}^{k-1} (k - i)I_{t+i}$$

Note that by relating *changes* in profits to investment, this technique nets out all inframarginal profits and rents on total assets and thus does provide the estimates of marginal returns on capital, which we seek.

The original BHMQ study divided investment into its three sources, ploughback, new debt and new equity, and made separate estimates of the returns on each. BHMQ experimented with different choices for k, for the lag between π and I, and for the definition of π (i.e., gross or net of depreciation). Although some sensitivity to these choices was observed, a fairly consistent pattern emerged across the various equations. "[T]he rate of return on equity capital is higher by a substantial margin than that on the other two forms of new capital. Depending on the lag involved, the rate of return on equity capital ranged from 14.5 percent to 20.8 percent. The rate of return on ploughback, however, ranged from 3.0 to 4.6 percent; while the rate of return on dept ranged from 4.2 to 14 percent. Thus, it appears that the rate of return on new equity is substantially higher than the rate of return on ploughback; while the rate of return on new debt is somewhere between the rates of return to ploughback and equity" (p. 353). Relevant to the question of whether capital is being allocated efficiently is both the relative differences in returns across the various sources of finance and the absolute level of the returns on ploughback. If reinvested cash flows during the fifties earned on average only a 3 to 4.6 percent return, then they earned substantially less than the return their shareholders could have obtained by buying the equity of other firms. Fisher and Lorie's (1964) estimates of returns on the market portfolio of common shares for the fifties are in the range from 13 to 18 percent.

Friend and Husic (1973) in commenting upon BHMQ's results note that the estimates are plagued by heteroscedasticity and that a substantial fraction of companies issue no equity. After eliminating heteroscedasticity, they find that the estimated returns are both higher than those of BHMQ and thus closer to shareholder opportunity costs and, more importantly, that *among the companies issuing new equity* no significant differences in the returns across the three sources of finance are found.

In responding to Friend and Husic, BHMQ note that it is not surprising to find that firms going to the equity market earn relatively high returns on ploughback, since it is presumably because they have high investment opportunities that they issue new equity. The original BHMQ hypothesis that the capital market does not effectively discipline managers' investment decisions is obviously most applicable to management's use of internal fund flows. Accordingly, BHMQ report estimates of the returns on ploughback for the sample of firms, *which did not issue any equity.* When book value of assets is used as a deflator to eliminate heteroscedasticity the returns to ploughback range from −1.1 to 11.2 percent. When the market value of the firm is used as a deflator, all estimates are negative.

The exchange between BHMQ and Friend and Husic makes it clear that there exist important differences in the returns on investment across firms. If firms in early phases of their life cycle make heavier reliance on the external capital market than mature companies then the BHMQ results would also tend to corroborate the life cycle hypothesis. Grabowski and I (1975) tested this hypothesis directly. We estimated returns on investment out of all sources of finance for firms, which were founded after World War II or predominantly sold products in the early phases of their life cycle. These estimated returns ranged from 13.7 percent to 26.3 percent for funds invested in the fifties and early-to-mid-sixties. In contrast, the range of estimates for mature firms was from 9.2 to 12.5 percent. Although the latter are higher than the returns BHMQ estimated, they are all below the Fisher and Lorie estimates of stock market returns.

John Hiller (1978) also compared his estimates of marginal rates of return on investment to the Fisher and Lorie stock market returns estimates. Depending on choice of depreciation rate, he found that from 57 to 68 percent of his sample of 144 companies had estimated marginal returns on investment significantly below the Fisher–Lorie index for five or more consecutive years over the fifties and sixties. His results, like those of BHMQ and Grabowski and Mueller, are inconsistent with the neoclassical theory of the firm as in Modigliani and Miller (1958), that assumes managers are constrained in their investment decisions to choose only projects earning rates of return at least as great as those available to their shareholders elsewhere.

The BHMQ article has been followed by studies for Canada and the UK. McFetridge's study of 205 large Canadian companies for the period 1961–70 is most comparable to BHMQ's in methodology (1978). He presents a range of estimates depending on lag structure chosen and on whether intercepts are included. In all 12 equations presented, the estimated returns on equity exceed those on plough-back with the differences being as large as 7.8 percent on plough-back as against 23.6 percent on equity. Nevertheless, the standard errors on the estimated coefficients are sufficiently large so that the differences between the coefficients on ploughback and new equity are typically insignificantly different from zero at the 5 percent level using two-tail tests (but not always if 10 percent level or one-tail tests are used). McFetridge concludes, "Managerial earnings retention policies are not a source of inefficiency" (p. 223).

While the differences in estimated returns on equity and plough-back in McFetridge's study are not statistically significant, they are economically significant. For the specification McFetridge favors (i.e. including an unweighted constant), his estimated returns on ploughback range between 2.7 percent and 6.8 percent. These returns must be considerably below what shareholders could have earned in the Canadian stock market during the sixties. That large absolute differences in coefficients prove to be statistically insig-nificant implies only that the standard errors of the coefficients are large, in turn implying that many firms earn even lower returns on ploughback than the average returns McFetridge reports. Given that this average is itself below the opportunity cost of capital for Canadian shareholders, McFetridge's study indicates rather clearly that many Canadian firms earn substantially lower returns on reinvested retained earnings than their shareholders could earn in the market. Certainly for the shareholders of these firms, man-agerial retention policies are a source of inefficiency.

Brealey, Hodge and Capron (1976) propose several modifications to the BHMQ estimating procedure and present estimates for 816 UK companies over the 1949–63 period. They note that new equity accounts on average for less than 1 percent of assets (p. 474). Moreover, most firms issue no new equity in a given year. Thus, it is not surprising that the standard errors on this variable's coefficients are large and it is difficult to establish statistically significant differences in estimated returns across sources of finance and they, like McFetridge, often find that the differences observed are not statistically significant. Moreover, the returns on plough-back occasionally exceed those on new equity.

Brealey, Hodges and Capron (1976) propose several modifications to the BHMQ estimating procedure and present estimates for 816 returns that should equal the cost of capital according to neoclassi-cal theory.[35] They therefore attempt to estimate true marginal

---

[35] BHMQ regress *changes* in profits on investment and thus do estimate a marginal return on total capital, albeit for large investments their estimates may also contain inframarginal rents. Should the latter occur, their estimates for a given firm would exceed the true marginal returns. Thus, if the BHMQ-type estimates are below the neoclassical cost of capital, as they are in the BHMQ, Grabowski and Mueller, and McFetridge studies, accurately measured marginal returns must *a fortiori* also be lower.

returns by controlling for the size of investment for each firm. They do this by first regressing returns on risk and the ratio of total investment to initial size and then regressing the residuals from this equation on the three sources of finance. The results from both stages are interesting. In accordance with neoclassical theory, Brealey *et al.* assume that "[i]f companies accept all projects with positive net present values, one might expect that the average return would be high when a large volume of projects is undertaken," but find "contrary to expectations, [that] the average return *declines* with the volume of investment" (p. 475, italics in original). "The second-stage results show sharp divergencies in the estimated returns on the different kinds of finance, with the return on new equity substantially and significantly higher than on plowback" (p. 475). Thus, the results from both stages of the Brealey, *et al.,* estimating procedures are inconsistent with neoclassical theory. But the authors cannot accept this implication. "Our reluctance to accept this finding stems from an unwillingness to accept the stage-one implications that companies either systematically overestimate the returns on large projects or require a lower return on them" (p. 475). But this reluctance is difficult to fathom. If managers do invest ploughback funds in projects with lower returns than their shareholders can earn elsewhere, then they are *not* using a criterion of accepting only those "projects with positive net present values." Moreover, the bigger the investment project the lower the returns on average will be. Brealey, *et al.*'s first stage results confirm still further what is apparent in their second stage results, that there is significant overinvestment out of ploughback among large companies. Brealey, *et al.* dismiss the plausibility of one set of results that are inconsistent with neoclassical theory, because they are obtained from another set of results that are inconsistent with neoclassical theory. In so doing, they illustrate nicely why it is that neoclassical theory remains so immune to empirical falsification.[36]

Geoffrey Whittington (1972, 1978) adopted a different methodology than BHMQ and thus his results for the UK are somewhat difficult to compare with theirs. By controlling for past profitability and growth he eliminates characteristics of the firm, which one

---

[36] For further discussion and evidence on this point, see Mueller (1984).

expects to be related to the relative profitability of their investment. His results nevertheless indicate small but statistically significant higher returns for those UK companies, which issued new equity.

The oil price rise in 1973 is the kind of shock to an economic system that often makes comparisons of the predictions of competing hypotheses easy. One assumes that the initial impact of the dramatic oil price increase of 1973 was to shift the marginal return on investment schedules for many firms far to the left. Investment in technologies that required relatively large oil inputs, or that manufactured complements to oil, like autos, became much less profitable. Of course, investment in technologies that substituted for oil would become more profitable, but for such a large price dislocation as occurred in 1973 it is doubtful that such technologies could have been sitting on the shelf in sufficient number to make a smooth transition possible. Thus, particularly taking into account the importance of the automobile in the U.S. economy, one expects in aggregate a leftward shift in the marginal return on investment schedule.

Assuming the cost of capital was not immediately affected, neoclassical theory predicts a sharp fall in investment and a dramatic increase in dividends, since current profit flows did not fall much. Given the latter, the managerial theory predicts no fall in investment, no increase in dividends, and a dramatic decline in the returns on investment as management continues to plough back current cash flows into technologies that have now become unprofitable, and that is exactly what occurred.

Figures on aggregate expenditures on plant in equipment reveal no deviation in their upward trend in 1973.[37] The first slowing of growth in investment is in 1975, a year of strong economic depression in which cash flows were down significantly. Estimates of

---

[37] Figures on total new plant and equipment expenditures for the relevant years are as follows (in billions of dollars):

1971	81
1972	88
1973	100
1974	112
1975	113
1976	120
1977	136

marginal returns on capital for a sample of 187 firms over this period have been made by Brainard, Shoven, and Weiss (1980).

> Comparison of the internal rate of return for the cash-out and constant-capital assumptions is also informative. . . Through 1969 the internal rate for the constant-capital case is always above the internal rate for the cash-out case. That is, the present value of the typical firm is higher if it remains in business and replaces capital as it wears out. From 1973 on, the internal rate is higher for the cash-out case— according to our calculations new investment is on average un-profitable at the discount rate implied in the valuation of existing capital (p. 477).

In fact, the real rate of return hovers around zero after 1973 (p. 477). Moreover, management not only did not respond to the oil price shock by increasing dividends, they sharply cut them (Hall, 1980, p. 507).

A firm whose internal fund flows exceed the set of investment projects promising returns equal to or greater than stockholder investment opportunities elsewhere will, according to neoclassical theory, return the extra funds to its shareholders through the issuance of dividends or repurchase of its outstanding shares. For a mature firm with limited investment opportunities, such a policy might imply that most of the company's cash flows are given away, and the company gradually shrinks in size as its markets decline. Few managers are likely to relish the thought of supervising the decline and dismantling of their firm. That they would use some of the cash over which they have discretion to avoid the company's decline in size is natural. Evidence that they do, if it exists, should be found in estimates of the marginal returns on investment across different companies.

The studies by BHMQ (1973), Grabowski and Mueller (1975), Hiller (1977, 1978), and Whittington (1972, 1978) indicate that different firms earn significantly different rates of return on invest-ment. The papers by BHMQ (1970, 1973), Grabowski and Mueller (1975), Hiller (1977, 1978), and McFetridge (1978) indicate that for many firms the return on their investment was significantly below the neoclassical cost of capital, even during an era of economic prosperity like the fifties and sixties. When prosperity turned to depression in 1973, the *mean* marginal return on investment for large firms fell to zero, as companies continued to plough back cash flows, and even cut dividends to do so (Brainard, *et al.*, 1980). These studies suggest that a substantial volume of investment occurs each year at returns significantly below the opportunity cost of capital. Unfortunately, by first posing the question of capital market efficiency as one of differences in returns across sources of finance rather than differences across types of firms, BHMQ diverted the profession's attention away from the central issues. Do some firms overinvest? If so, what are their characteristics? While the results reviewed in this section suggest answers to these questions, more research specifically directed at answering them is clearly needed.

H. The effects of mergers

Mergers are the quickest way to grow and the most popular avenue to diversification (Berry, 1975; Scherer and Ravenscraft, 1984). Mergers are highly visible, lumpy investment decisions, whose effects on company size, growth, and profitability ought to be easy to determine. Unfortunately, they are not. There are several reasons for this. First, many of the acquired companies are small and/or privately owned and thus do not publish income and balance sheet data. Thus, it is impossible to adjust for the acquisition's effect on the acquiring firm's profitability and size. Second, even when both companies are public, a variety of accounting conventions are used to combine the income and balance sheet data of the merging companies. Readjusting the data to make them comparable across firms is no easy task. Nor is it made easier by the firms themselves. Although one expects that corporate management does maintain separate income and balance sheet records of its acquisitions for at least the first few years after they occur, and for diversification mergers indefinitely, companies virtually never publish separate income and balance sheet statements for their acquisitions which would allow one to determine how successful the acquisitions have been. Indeed, demands from security regulation and antitrust authorities for the publication of accounting data by industry or product line, the kind of data that would make monitoring the effects of diversification mergers rather easy, have been resisted most strenuously by corporate managers. These difficulties with accounting data have led many to turn to stock

market data to evaluate mergers effects. But these data have their
limitations also, as we shall see.

1. *Mergers' effects on concentration*

Perhaps the most widely discussed and debated consequence of
mergers is their effect on concentration. Interest in this question
arose in the United States at the turn of the century when the first
great wave of mergers took place (see Figure 1) and many of the
great trusts were created. No one questions that this merger wave
led to a substantial increase in both overall and industry concentration levels, although the data do not allow this increase to be
quantified (Markham, 1955; Stigler, 1950).

The second major merger wave in the United States occurred
during the late 1920s. It coincided with a substantial increase in

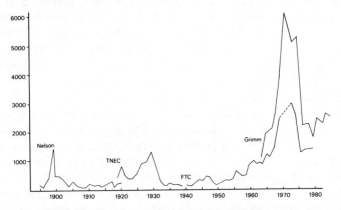

Sources: The 1895–1968 observations are for manufacturing and mining mergers
and acquisitions. The 1895–1920 observations are from "Merger Movements in
American Industry, 1895–1956" by Ralph L. Nelson. The 1919–39 observations are
from "The Structure of American Industry," Monograph No. 27, Temporary
National Economic Committee. The 1940–68 and 1972–79 observations are from the
Bureau of Economics, Federal Trade Commission. Note that the 1972–79 observations are the number of completed acquisitions for all asset sizes in manufacturing,
mining, wholesale and retail trade, services and others, and those companies whose
industry classification is unknown. The 1963–84 observations are from W. T. Grimm
& Co. W. T. Grimm & Co. tabulations measure only publicly announced
transactions and include transfers of ownership of ten percent or more of a
company's assets or equity, provided that the value of the transaction is at least
$500,000.

FIGURE 1A   Number of merger and acquisition transactions.

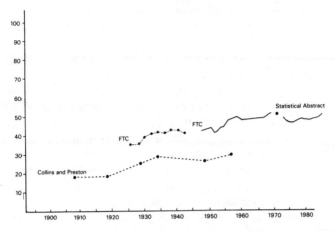

Sources: The 1909–59 percentages are for total assets of the 100 largest manufacturing, mining, and distribution corporations. These percentages are for Norman Collins and Lee Preston, "The Size Structure of the Largest Industry Firms," *American Economic Review,* December 1961. The 1925–82 percentages are for manufacturing assets accounted for by the 100 largest firms. The 1925–41 and 1947–68 observations are from the Federal Trade Commission *Economic Report on Corporate Mergers,* 1969. The 1963–82 observations are from the *1984 Statistical Abstract.*

FIGURE 1B   Aggregate concentration overtime.

overall concentration (see Figure 1). George Stigler has named this wave, the wave to create oligopoly, and in many industries it did (1950). Were data available at the industry level, they would undoubtedly also show substantial increases in concentration in the late twenties.

Data are not available to measure overall concentration during the war years of the early forties, but a slight increase in overall concentration during the merger "ripple" of the late forties is apparent (Markham's term, 1955). Overall concentration climbs steeply during the fifties and merger activity also begins its long ascendance, crescendoing in the late sixties. The rise in concentration during the fifties comes too soon and seems too steep to be attributable entirely to mergers. But John McGowan (1965), in the only systematic investigation of the effects of mergers on concentration in the United States published to date, calculated that concentration would not have risen at all had there been no mergers in the fifties. He predicted a decline in overall concentration during the sixties in the absence of mergers. But there were mergers in the sixties, a great many of them, and aggregate concentration crept upward (see Table IV).

Several writers have noted that overall concentration flattened out during much of the sixties, even though merger activity was quite high, and thus dismiss the importance of mergers to the aggregate concentration issue (White, 1982; Hay and Untiet, 1981). The fact that overall concentration held steady during much of the sixties, in spite of the large volume of assets acquired, is itself a revealing fact, however, Acquiring firms are on average much larger than other companies (Mueller, 1980, pp. 299–302). From 1960 through 1969, the 200 largest companies acquired a cumulative amount of assets equivalent to 12.2 percent of their size at the time of acquisition (Mueller, 1979, p. 812). That these acquisitions did not result in a corresponding increase in aggregate concentration can only imply that the internal growth rates of the largest 200 companies were less than the growth in assets for the manufacturing sector.

The latter is what one expects if the largest companies in the economy are in the mature phases of their life cycle. The same phenomenon explains why these firms resorted to mergers to achieve growth and why these mergers did not result in a greater increase in concentration than they did. The fifties and sixties were a period of unprecedented economic growth and prosperity in the United States. Thousands of new firms were born and many grew to considerable size. That this period of prosperity was not accompanied by a relative decline in the importance of the largest firms is due to a considerable extent to the offsetting effects of mergers.

This inference is confirmed in the unpublished Ph.D. dissertation of Philip Spilberg (1985). He has examined the effect of mergers on concentration using a sample of 14,676 companies in manufacturing, mining, transportation, wholesaling and retailing. His calculations actually reveal a slight decline in aggregate concentration between 1959 and 1978 (see Table VI). This decline is brought about by the entry of new firms, some 864,000, over the twenty year period. Counteracting the new entry of firms is the Gibrat effect (differences in internal growth rates across firms) and mergers in roughly equal proportions. In the absence of mergers, the 100 largest firms in 1978 would have controlled 14 percent less assets

TABLE VI

Change in aggregate concentration, 1959–1978

	1959 distribution	Percent change due to new entry[a]	Percent change due to internal growth	Percent change due to entry & growth	Percent change due to merger activity	Total percent change	Total absolute change	1978 distribution
Variance of logarithms	4.244	n.a.	1.1%	n.a.	n.a.	−2.9%	−0.123	4.121
Herfindahl index[b]	0.230	−52.8%	8.8%	−44.0%	21.0%	−23.0%	−0.053	0.177
50 firm concentration ratio	0.238	−31.4%	11.4%	−20.1%	11.2%	−8.8%	−0.021	0.217
100 firm concentration ratio	0.308	−31.4%	8.8%	−22.6%	14.1%	−8.5%	−0.026	0.282
200 firm concentration ratio	0.373	−31.4%	9.8%	−21.7%	16.3%	−5.3%	−0.020	0.353

[a] Assumes an entry firm distribution with a standard deviation twice the size of the mean.
[b] Actual Herfindahl indices (such as 0.00230) have been multiplied by 100 to provide greater detail.
Source: Spilberg, 1985, p. 179.

than they actually did. Since 1978, levels of merger activity have accelerated and concentration has again risen (see Figure 1 and Table IV).

Mergers have had a similar effect on overall concentration in the United Kingdom. Hannah and Kay (1977) have analyzed the effects of mergers on concentration in the UK up through 1970. Table VII presents figures for the share of output accounted for by the 100 largest firms in various years and the numbers of companies disappearing because of mergers over the preceding five years. The two move closely together. Only in the immediate post-World War II period does concentration increase significantly without a corresponding rise in mergers (see 1948 and 1953). (A similar phenomenon occurred in the United States.) Note in particular the substantial increase in concentration between 1919 and 1930 accompanied by an acceleration in merger activity and the subsequent decline in both concentration and merger activity from 1930 to 1948. Essentially the same pattern emerged in the United States. Hannah and Kay conclude as John McGowan's and Philip Spilberg's analyses indicate for the United States, that overall concentration in the UK would have declined since World War II had it not been for the effects of mergers.

TABLE VII
Concentration and merger activity in the UK, 1909–1970

Year	Share of 100 largest in manufacturing net output	Number of firm disappearances over five previous years
1909	0.15	165
1919	0.17	272
1924	0.21	893
1930	0.26	1,150
1935	0.23	556
1039	0.23	883
1948	0.21	462
1953	0.26	525
1958	0.33	919
1963	0.38	2,114
1968	0.42	3,048
1970	0.45	2,876

Source: Hannah and Kay, 1977.

2. Mergers' effects on efficiency

More important for the issue of capital market efficiency is the effect of mergers on the efficiency of the merging companies. If mergers increase economic efficiency, then constant or rising industrial concentration may be defended as a necessary consequence of the Darwinian forces at work in a competitive economy.

Mergers can increase corporate efficiency in a variety of ways. Simplest of all to understand is a horizontal merger between two firms of less than minimum efficient size. But cost reductions have also been claimed as a consequence of vertical or conglomerate expansion.[38] With respect to conglomerate mergers, it has also been argued that they can reduce a company's cost of capital by reducing the riskiness of its investments (Lintner, 1971), or by creating an internal capital market that is more efficient than the external capital market (Weston, 1970; Williamson, 1970). To the extent that mergers reduce a company's cost of capital investment, R and D, and advertising are stimulated. While capital investment and R and D can lower costs, they can also lead to quality improvements and advertising can change buyer perceptions of quality. Thus, in the long run mergers can affect consumer welfare by changing either costs or quality.

These effects of mergers can be illustrated with the following simple model.[39] Assume a monopolistically competitive industry of n firms in which each firm i faces a demand schedule

$$p_i = a_i - bx_i - b\sigma \sum_{j \neq i}^{n} x_j. \tag{1}$$

All firm demand schedules have the same slopes, but the intercepts differ with higher a_is signifying a greater willingness to pay for each unit of output on the part of consumers due to a perceived higher quality. Product differentiation is parameterized by σ ($0 \leq \sigma \leq 1$), where ($\sigma = 0$) implies a pure monopoly, ($\sigma = 1$) a homogeneous product.

Let differences in efficiency across firms be represented by

---

[38] For surveys of this literature, see Steiner (1975, ch. 3); Mueller (1977b); Scherer (1980, pp. 133–38); Hughes, Mueller, and Singh in (Mueller, 1980, ch. 2).

[39] This model is developed in detail and the following results derived in Mueller (1986, chs. 4, 9).

differing unit costs c_i, where total costs are defined as $TC_i = c_i x_i$. Then profits, π_i are

$$\pi_i = (p_i - c_i)x_i$$

Possible collusion among firms in the industry is represented by the parameter θ in each firm's objective function

$$O_i = \pi_i + \theta \sum_{j \neq i}^{n} \pi_j \tag{2}$$

where $\theta = 1$ implies perfect collusion, $\theta = 0$ Cournot independence, and $\theta = 1/(n-1)$ Bertrand rivalry. Maximizing (2) with respect to x_i and considerable algebra yield

$$x_i = (1 + r)q_i - rQ + r^2(n-2)X, \tag{3}$$

where $q_i = (a_i - c_i)/2b$, $r = \sigma(1 + \theta)/2$, $Q = \sum_l^n q_i$ and $X = \sum_l^n x_i = Q/(nr - r + 1)$. Division of (3) by X and more algebra yields an expression for market share, m_i,

$$m_i = \frac{x_i}{X} = \frac{q_i(nr - r + 1)}{(1-r)Q} - \frac{r}{(1-r)} \tag{4}$$

Higher q implies a greater gap between i's product quality parameter a_i and its unit costs c_i. Larger q_i implies larger market shares.

$$\frac{\partial m_i}{\partial q_i} = \frac{nr - r + 1}{(1-r)Q} - \frac{(nr - r + 1)q_i}{(1-r)Q^2} = \frac{(Q - q_i)(nr - r + 1)}{(1-r)Q^2} > 0 \tag{5}$$

A merger which improves the quality of the merging companies' product mix relative to their unit costs expands their market share.

Only two studies have made direct estimates of the effects of mergers on market shares. Goldberg (1973) measured changes in market shares for 44 companies concentrated in markets with heavy advertising. He tracked the merging companies for one to eleven years after the merger. He found no significant change in their market shares following the mergers.

Mueller (1985; 1986, ch. 9) examined the market shares of companies acquired in conglomerate mergers between 1950 and 1972 and pairs of companies engaged in horizontal mergers during the same years. The changes in market shares for these firms between 1950 and 1972 were compared with those of nonmerging companies in the same industries. The companies acquired through conglomerate mergers or involved in horizontal mergers were found to have experienced significant losses in market shares following the mergers relative to nonmerging companies. For example, while the average nonacquired company had a 1972 market share that was 88.5 percent of its 1950 value, the average company acquired through a conglomerate merger had a 1972 market share of only 18 percent of its 1950 value.

Where market share data are unavailable an indirect test of whether mergers have increased efficiency can be made by seeing whether the merging companies increased their overall size relative to similar companies following the mergers. This test was conducted for merging pairs of companies in 7 countries.[40] In each case a merging pair was matched to a pair of nonmerging firms of similar size to the merging pair and drawn from the same industry(ies). The growth rates of the merging and control group companies were measured over the five years preceding the merger and the three or five years (depending on data availability) after the merger. In no country did the merging firms exhibit an increase in their internal growth rates relative to the control group firms in the years following the mergers. In Holland and the United States, there was a statistically significant relative decline in growth.

Two additional studies of mergers in the United States, Hogarty (1970b) and Lev and Mandelker (1972), observed either lower than predicted sales or slower internal growth rates for merging firms following the mergers. These findings regarding post-merger sales and growth rates are consistent with those of Goldberg and Mueller using market shares. Eleven separate studies spanning seven countries have failed to find any evidence of increased internal efficiency based on sales data. Five of the eleven have presented evidence suggesting a decline in efficiency.

3. *Mergers' effects on profitability*

If mergers increase efficiency, they should increase profitability. Improvement in product quality following a merger should allow

---

[40] The countries were Belgium, the Federal Republic of Germany, France, the Netherlands, Sweden, the United Kingdom, and the United States.

higher prices to be charged and lead to higher profits. Another test for the efficiency effects of mergers is to see whether they have increased profitability.

Increased profitability is a necessary but not sufficient condition for the inference that mergers have increased efficiency. Profits could rise following a merger because it had lessened competition within a market or, at least, so it was thought until a recent paper by Salant, Switzer, and Reynolds (1983) appeared. They demonstrated that a horizontal merger among two competitors in a homogeneous product industry does not increase the combined profits of the merging firms. To see the logic behind their result, let us modify the model developed above. Let $\sigma = 1$, to represent a homogeneous product, and industry demand be given as

$$P = A - BX \tag{6}$$

Each of the n firms in the industry then faces a demand schedule

$$P_i = A - \frac{B}{n} x_i - \frac{B}{n} \sum_{j \neq i}^{n} x_j \tag{7}$$

If all firms have the same unit costs C, then substitution into (2) and maximization with respect to x_i yields

$$x_i = \frac{(A - C)}{B(1 + n + \theta n - \theta)} \tag{8}$$

from which (9) is obtained as the expression for the profits of any one of the identical sized firms in an industry of n firms.

$$\pi_n = \frac{(A - C)^2 (1 + \theta n - \theta)}{B(1 + n + \theta n - \theta)^2} \tag{9}$$

A further dose of algebra applied to (9) reveals that $2\pi_n > \pi_{n-1}$ for all $n > 2$ when $\theta \geq 0$. Thus, in the absence of changes in efficiency and the degree of cooperation, θ, two firms in a homogeneous product industry with $\theta \geq 0$ never find it profitable to merge.

While this result first strikes one as counter intuitive, a moment's reflection reveals the intuition behind the result. It relies heavily on the assumption that the equilibrium both *before and after* the merger is symmetric with each firm of equal size. A horizontal merger can then be thought of as composed of two steps. First, the production capacity of one of the merging firms is retired so that there are now $n - 1$ equal sized firms in the industry. Second, all $n - 1$ firms adjust their outputs symmetrically to the new level implied by (8) with the number of firms now being $n - 1$. In the new equilibrium, each firm's profits are greater than before the merger, i.e., $\pi_{n-1} > \pi_n$, but the increase in profits to a single firm in going from an n firm to an $n - 1$ firm equilibrium is never large enough to offset the loss of profits from retiring the production capacity of one of the merging firms.

Casual observation suggests that mergers seldom result in the retirement of all of the productive capacity of a merger partner and thus one can anticipate that a horizontal merger leaves the merging companies bigger than their rivals. If one assumes that the post-merger equilibrium is one in which the profits of the industry equal those that would arise from an $n - 1$ firm symmetric equilibrium, but that the merged company is double the size of the other $n - 2$ equal-sized firms, then the merger is profitable. Alternatively, if one assumes that there is product differentiation, so that both of the products of the merging firms continue to be produced, then the merger can also result in higher profits for the merging firms.[41] And, of course, the traditional concern of antitrust authorities has been with the possibility that mergers facilitate cooperation within an industry, i.e., increase θ. Changes in θ increase industry profits and can make unprofitable mergers profitable even in the symmetric equilibrium cases. In any event, we know that mergers do in fact occur and often in amazingly large numbers. Our concern now is whether they are *ex post* profitable.

Several studies of the first two merger waves in the United States exist.[42] Although severely dated as judged by today's statistical standards, the results are sufficiently consistent across studies that one can draw with some confidence at least one conclusion as to the effect of these early mergers on profitability. It is that they did not lead to increases in profitability on average. Some students of this

---

[41] On this and other points raised in this paragraph, see Perry and Porter (1985).

[42] Markham (1955), Nelson (1959), Reid (1968), Eis (1969), Hogarty (1970a), and references therein.

period even believe that the merging companies' profits fell following the mergers. This conclusion is somewhat remarkable because the first two merger waves in the United States took place at a time when horizontal and vertical acquisitions were allowed. Many companies were created which had dominant market positions at that time and have remained dominant until today. It is difficult to believe that some of these mergers did not result in sufficient increases in market power to generate extra profits. The reductions in profits due to losses in efficiency among the other mergers were apparently sufficiently great to offset these gains, however.

Weston and Mansinghka (1971) were among the first to study the profitability effects of post-World War II mergers. They focussed upon a sample of 63 companies that were active acquirers during the sixties, companies whose diversification through merger strategies made them symbols of the conglomerate merger movement. Weston and Mansinghka found that these active acquirers had significantly lower profit rates (e.g. before tax profits over total assets equal to 0.087) than did a randomly selected sample of industrials (0.167) prior to the conglomerates' launching onto their acquisition programs in the sixties. These characteristics of the Weston–Mansinghka sample make it ideal for testing whether diversification by mature companies with limited opportunities for internal expansion improves economic efficiency. Indeed, Weston and Mansinghka call the merger strategies of these firms "defensive diversification" in recognition of the likelihood that it is the below normal performance of these firms in their base industries that induces them to diversify.

Unfortunately, Weston and Mansinghka do not test whether the acquisition programs of the conglomerates resulted in enhanced efficiency. Instead they compare the profit rates of the conglomerates to those of the control group of industrials after the conglomerates have engaged in a decade of intensive merger activity. Weston and Mansinghka find the mean return on assets of the conglomerates at the later date (0.151) to be nearly equal to that of the industrials (0.156). They conclude that the conglomerates' managements are capable of "preserving the values of ongoing organizations as well as restoring the earning power of the entities" (p. 928).

But this conclusion is misleading.[43] When a firm with below average profitability acquires another, the acquired firm is likely to have a higher profit rate than its acquirer. Indeed, if it is its below average profitability that motivates the acquirer to make acquisitions, the acquirer is almost certain to seek out firms more profitable than itself and Melicher and Rush (1974) report that the companies the Weston–Mansinghka conglomerates acquired were indeed significantly more profitable than their acquirers. The combined profit rate of the two merging firms must, then, be higher than the acquiring firms's initial profit rate, unless the merger causes a fall in the acquired firm's profitability to the level of the acquirer. After a decade of merger activity on the scale of the Weston–Mansinghka sample of conglomerates, the simple arithmetic of averaging could "restore" the conglomerates' profit rate to the average of other firms without any improvement in the efficiency of any of the merging partners having taken place.

I attempted to adjust for the averaging effect of mergers by regressing the long run projected profit rates for a sample of 551 companies on both the volume of assets they acquired from 1950 through 1972 and their profit rate at the start of the sample period (1986, ch. 8). I found evidence of a significant averaging effect due to mergers. Companies with below average profits in 1950 had their long run profit rates raised in direct proportion to the volume of assets they acquired. Companies with profits initially above the average had their profit rates reduced in proportion to the volume of assets they acquired. Once one controlled for averaging effect of mergers, no residual synergistic effect on profits was found. In one specification of the model, a small *negative* effect of mergers on profitability (significant at the 10 percent level) was even observed.

The proper way to test whether mergers have generated additional profits is to measure the profits of the merging companies

---

[43] It is also controverted in a follow-up study by Melicher and Rush (1974). The Weston and Mansinghka data measure post-merger profitability in 1968, near the peak of a business cycle. In making their acquisitions, the conglomerates often issued debt so that in 1968 they were much more highly levered than the industrial firms to which they were compared. Melicher and Rush (1974) found no superiority in the performance of the conglomerate firms when compared to industrial companies, over the business cycle peak years of the late sixties, and through the years of the early seventies.

prior to the merger and afterwards and see whether the latter have increased. This test was conducted for a sample of 280 mergers over the period 1962–72. To control for other factors that might effect profitability before and after the mergers, the profit changes for the merging pairs were compared with those of a control group sample matched to both the acquiring firm and the acquired firm in terms of both size and industry, and to the mean levels of the industries in which the acquiring and the acquired firms were chiefly operating. Merging firms were found to have changes in pretax profitability between the five years preceding the merger and the three years after, which were insignificantly different from the changes observed for the control group firms over the same time intervals. A small, but significant, increase in after-tax profits in comparison with the control group firms was observed, however. Comparisons of both pre- and post-tax profit rates between merging companies and their base industries tended to yield insignificant differences. Although the post-tax increases in profits relative to the control group are consistent with a profit motive for the mergers, it is the pre-tax rates that are relevant for assessing economic efficiency gains. Here no evidence exists for this sample of 280 mergers between 1962 and 1972, that they resulted in any increase in profits and *a fortiori* in efficiency (Mueller, 1980, ch. 9).

The same methodology was used to examine the effects of mergers on profitability in six European countries. The results were sometimes sensitive to whether comparison was with the size and industry matched control group companies or the industries from which the merging companies were drawn and to whether pre- or post-tax profit rates were used. But, the pattern of results was sufficiently consistent within any given country to allow one to conclude that in three countries (Belgium, the Federal Republic of Germany, and the United Kingdom) mergers either had no effect on profitability or led to slight increases. In the other three countries (France, Holland, and Sweden) profits either declined slightly following the mergers or were unchanged (Mueller, 1980, chs. 3–8, 10). As with the results in the United States for the first two merger waves, the significance of these results for Europe arises in that a more consistent and dramatic positive effect of mergers on profitability has not been observed. Had profit increases been observed in all countries, one would still be left with the question of interpreting whether they were due to market power or efficiency increases. That horizontal mergers reduce market power seems unlikely. Thus, one must conclude that in three countries efficiency seems on average to have declined by enough to offset or more than offset any beneficial increases in market power for the mergers. In Belgium, West Germany, and the United Kingdom, the efficiency losses of some firms following the mergers, if there were any, were on average smaller or no greater than the gains in market power for the other merging firms in the sample. Here the results of the previous section should be recalled. If mergers improve the efficiency of the merger partners, their costs fall and their sales should expand relative to other firms. In none of the three countries in which there is evidence of an increase in profitability following the mergers is there evidence of a relative increase in sales. Thus, the increases in profitability in these countries do not appear to be predominately due to efficiency gains.

The most exhaustive study of merger effects on profitability conducted to date is by David J. Ravenscraft and F. M. Scherer (forthcoming). They have gathered data on roughly 6,000 lines of business (a company's operations in a single industry) acquired between 1950 and 1977. Preliminary results indicate slight if any improvement in the profit to assets ratios of the acquired companies, when assets are measured at pre-acquisition book values, and significant declines in returns when acquired assets are restated as the purchase price of the acquired company. Ravenscraft and Scherer find that acquired companies are more profitable than otherwise similar nonacquired firms, and that their profitability declines steadily after they are acquired.

The most exhaustive published study of the effects of mergers on profitability by anyone to date is by Geoffrey Meeks (1977). Meeks' study deserves special attention because of the number of mergers studied, more than 1000, and the care he took to adjust the basic accounting data to make the observations comparable. Meeks concluded that mergers in the United Kingdom have resulted on average in modest *declines* in profitability.

Similar to Meeks' study in terms of labor input but different in methodology are the case studies of individual mergers in the United Kingdom by Cowling and his associates (1979). These studies are revealing in demonstrating how mergers can increase efficiency and in developing a methodology for testing for such. But no consistent pattern regarding changes in efficiency is apparent in the mergers in these group studies.

No study in the United States has presented evidence suggesting that mergers increase profitability, which can be interpreted as consistent with there having been an increase in efficiency. Weston and Mansinghka make claims to such an effect, but their claims are unjustified since they did not allow for the averaging effect of mergers, and are contradicted by Melicher and Rush's follow-up study (1974). I have found some evidence of tax savings due to mergers, but found before tax profits to be either unchanged or lower depending on the comparison made (1980, ch. 9). The latter result combined with there having been a significant decline in the growth rate in sales of the merging firms cannot be reconciled with the conclusion that efficiency has increased. The massive study by Ravenscraft and Scherer (forthcoming) contains considerable evidence in contradiction with the hypothesis that the profitability of acquired firms is improved by their acquisition. All other evidence based on accounting data for the United States also points in the same direction.

The two largest investigations of mergers in the United Kingdom reach opposite conclusions. Meeks (1977) finds a slight decline in profitability in a study of 1000 mergers occurring since World War II; Cosh, Hughes, and Singh (Mueller, 1980, ch. 8) find a slight increase for 290 mergers occurring in the three years 1967–69. Studies of mergers in Belguim, West Germany, France, Holland, and Sweden paint an equally inconsistent picture. If mergers improve the operating performance of the merging companies, it is not readily apparent from the evidence available in studies using accounting data.

4. Mergers' effects on shareholder returns

a. *The findings.* During the 1960s, two independent developments took place, one real, one intellectual. On the intellectual front, pioneering papers in finance by Sharpe (1964) and Lintner (1965) demonstrated that, when shareholders hold diversified portfolios, the proper measure of a security's risk is not the variance of its return, but the covariance with the portfolio of all stocks. More accurately, it is the $\hat{\beta}$ estimated from a linear regression of firm i's returns, R_i, on the returns on the market portfolio, R_m.

At the same time that interest among scholars of finance was turning to questions of portfolio diversification, the measurement of risk, and more generally the efficiency of the capital market, the merger wave that began in the fifties was picking up steam. More and more mergers were taking place, and given the Supreme Court's tough interpretation of Section 7 of the Clayton Act, as amended in 1950, these mergers were increasingly oriented toward diversification. As the pace of mergers quickened, interest on Wall Street and in Congress in the efficiency properties of these mergers rose. Given the capital asset pricing model's (CAPM) focus upon diversification and capital market efficiency, it seemed an ideal analytic tool to answer these questions, and many from the finance field were quick to try to apply it to this end.

Although the development of the CAPM at the time of the great conglomerate merger wave in the United States in the sixties may seem sufficiently fortuitous to suggest that the marriage between research on mergers and finance must have been made in heaven, application of the CAPM to the study of mergers is not without its difficulties. The theory asserts that today's share price reflects the present discounted value of a firm's expected earnings' stream, and its risk characteristics. A merger could well affect either of these, but the exact magnitude and timing of the effects must be difficult to determine at the time the merger is announced. If this is true, then the "effects" of a merger to the extent that they are correctly forecasted and reflected in share prices are not completely evidenced at the time the merger is announced or even finalized. A "timing" problem is present, which may be both serious and vary from firm to firm. Of course, to the extent that the market has "rational expectations" with regard to mergers, over- and underestimates of future effects may wash out and the average future effects of mergers be accurately reflected in the average changes in share prices at the time of the mergers. But, the stock market is notorious for being bullish and bearish about the future at different points of time, and thus current prices do not always appear to be accurate reflections of future earnings (Shiller, 1981, 1984). Since merger activity is positively correlated with stock price swings,[44] it is possible that price changes surrounding mergers are not accurate reflections of future profit swings. Prudence would suggest tracking the share price behavior of merging firms for some time following the merger to determine whether any systematic revisions of the market's expectations as to the effects of the mergers occur.

The necessity to observe share price over some time span to measure merger effects creates the problem that other factors may intervene to obscure the effects of the mergers. A related problem is that acquiring firms are often much larger than the firms they acquire, so that anticipated changes can be expected to have but negligible effects upon share prices. For these, and other reasons[45] estimates of merger effects based upon stockholder returns must be viewed with some caution. But because these estimates are based on the expected future effects rather than on only realized effects, they do avoid the handicap of most other effects of mergers studies, which only measure the effects over a few years following the merger.[46]

Given diversification's negative effect on portfolio risk, a seemingly obvious motive for a diversification merger is to reduce risk, and several early papers in the finance literature rationalized conglomerate mergers in this way.[47] The theoretical proposition is now firmly established in the literature, however, that shareholder risk can be more efficiently reduced through portfolio diversification than through real asset diversification within a corporation (Levy and Sarnat, 1970; Smith, 1970; Azzi, 1978; Galai and Masulis, 1976; Higgins and Schall, 1975). Empirical research has also confirmed that portfolios of shares or mutual funds generally

---

[44] See evidence of Nelson (1959, 1966), Melicher, Ledolter, and D'Antonio (1983); and Geroski (1984).

[45] Several studies now exist critiquing the CAPM in general, and its use in merger studies in particular. The efficient share portfolio is not one in which each listed share is held in proportion to its share of the market portfolio, but one in which *negative* positions in many shares are held (Roll, 1977; Levy, 1983). The relevance of the covariance of a share with the market portfolio is thus clouded. Moreover, mergers can be expected to change βs making use of the CAPM to analyze mergers particularly difficult (Brenner and Downes, 1979).

[46] But Goldberg (1973) had up to 11 years of post-merger data in his study of mergers effects on market shares, I had as many as 23 years (1985, 1986, ch. 9), and Ravenscraft and Scherer (forthcoming) have up to 28 years.

[47] Lintner (1971) and Lewellen (1971).

outperform conglomerate diversification (Smith and Schreiner, 1969; Mason and Goudzwaard, 1976). A major exception to this pattern would appear to be Weston, Smith, Shrieves (1972). They observed superior risk/return performance for a subset of 48 of the 63 conglomerates in the Weston–Mansinghka (1971) study, as compared to 50 mutual funds. But, as with the Weston–Mansinghka paper, the Weston–Smith–Shrieves results must be discounted because they measure conglomerate performance only over the upswing of the 1960s' bull market. The mean β for the Weston–Smith–Shrieves conglomerate sample was 1.928 compared with a mean β for their mutual fund control group of only 0.878. Thus, every one percentage point rise in the returns on the market portfolio during the sixties boom resulted in nearly a two percentage increase in conglomerate returns, while the mutual funds returns went up by less than 0.9 of a percentage point. The sharp decline in the stock market in the early seventies, immediately after the Weston–Smith–Shrieves' sample period, could be expected to result in greater declines for the conglomerates than for the mutual funds. Reid (1971) reported a much larger drop in returns (56 percent) for Weston and Mansinghka's sample of conglomerates than occurred for their industrials' sample between 1968 and mid-1970. Presumably the decline in price of the conservatively managed mutual funds was also substantially less than 56%. Moreover, no study has ever reported a significant reduction in risk, as measured by company β, as a result of conglomerate mergers. Lev and Mandelker (1972), Joehnk and Nielsen (1974), Dodd and Ruback (1977), and Magenheim and Mueller (forthcoming) all find that mergers have no systematic effect on company βs. If mergers improve company efficiency or market power, then these effects must be evidenced in increased rates of return on company shares.

Table VIII summarizes the rate of return evidence from 22 studies. They differ in time period, country of origin, and control group. A few studies, which might have been included, have been omitted because they employed the same sample as an included study (e.g., Jarrell and Bradley, 1980), or because they tested alternative hypotheses so that a comparison of their results with those included was difficult (e.g., Eckbo, 1983). With these exceptions, the included list represents a fairly exhaustive sampling of existing studies of the effects of mergers on shareholder returns. To

TABLE VIII
Returns to acquiring and acquired firm's shareholders

Study	Time period (country)	Returns prior to merger announcement, acquiring firms	Returns in announcement day (d) month (m), year (y) acquiring firm	Post-merger returns in days (d), months (m), years (y) after merger acquiring firms[a]	Acquired firms' returns	Sample	Control group
Hogarty (1970b)	1953–64 (USA)			−0.05 (y varies from +1 to +11)		43 nonconglomerates engaged in heavy merger activity	Firms in acquiring company's base industry
Lev and Mandelker (1972)	1952–63 (USA)	0.135[b] (y = −5, −1)	0.083 (y = 0)	0.056 (y = +1 to +5)		69 firms making large acquisitions	Nonmerging firms matched by industry and size
Halpern (1973)	1950–65 (USA)		0.063 (m = −7, 0)[e]		0.304 (m = −7 to 0)[e]	78 mergers by nonconglomerates	Market portfolio
Mandelker (1974)	1941–63 (USA)	0.048[b] (m = −34, −1)	0.003[b] (m = 0, 6)	−0.015[b] (m = 7, 46)	0.120*	241 large mergers	Market portfolio
Ellert (1976)	1950–72 (USA)	0.233* (m = −100 to −1)[c]	−0.018*[d]	−0.016 (m = +1, 48)		205 mergers challenged by Justice Dept. or FTC between 1950 and 1972	Market portfolio
Franks, Broyles, Hecht (1977)	1955–72 (UK)	−0.048 (m = −40, −1)	0.001 (m = 0)	−0.014 (m = 1, 2)	0.179	70 mergers by breweries and distilleries	Market portfolio
Dodd & Ruback (1977)	1958–78 (USA)	0.117* (m = −60, −1)	0.028 (m = 0)	−0.059[b] (m = 1, 60)	0.206*	136 tender offers	Market portfolio

Study	Period (Country)					Sample	Benchmark
Kummer & Hoffmeister (1978)	1956–74 (USA)	0.170^b (m = −40, −1)	0.052^b (m = 0)	0.006^b (m = 1, 20)	0.187*	88 cash tender offers	Market portfolio
Langetieg (1978)	1929–69 (USA)	0.136* (m = −64 to −1)	−0.028 (m = 0 to +5)	−0.262 (m = +7 to 78)	0.128*	149 mergers of all kinds	Market portfolio and industry index
Bradley (1980)	1962–77 (USA)		0.04* (d = 0, 5)	0.01^b (d = 6, 40)	0.36* − 0.49*	161 tender offers	Market portfolio
Dodd (1980)	1971–77 (USA)		−0.011 (d = −1, 0)	−0.072* (d = −10, 140)^f	0.340*	71 mergers	Market portfolio
Kumps & Wterwulghe (1980)	1962–74 (Belgium)		−0.047 (y = 0)	−0.014 (y = 1, 3)		26 mergers of all kinds	26 nonmerging firms matched by industry
Jenny & Weber (1980)	1962–72 (France)		0.116* (y = 0)	-0.095^b (y = 1, 3)		43 mergers of all kinds	43 nonmerging firms matched by size and industry
Ryden & Edberg (1980)	1962–76 (Sweden)		−0.040 (y = 0)	0.011^b (y = 1, 3)		23 mergers of all kinds	23 nonmerging firms
Cosh, Hughes & Singh (1980)	1967–69 (UK)	0.069* (y = −5, 1)	0.187* (y = +1)	-0.169^b (y = 1, 5)		63 mergers of all kinds	63 nonmerging firms matched by size and industry
Mueller (1980)	(1962–72) (USA)		0.088* (y = 0)	-0.084^b (y = 1, 3)		219 mergers of all kinds	219 nonmerging firms matched by size and industry
Firth (1980)	1969–75 (UK)	0.014^b (m = −480, −1)	−0.063 (m = 0)	0.001^b (m = 1, 36)	0.363	434 mergers of all kinds	Market portfolio
Asquith (1983)	1962–72 (USA)	0.132^b (d = −480, −1)	0.002 (m = 0)	−0.072* (d = 1, 240)	0.133*	196 mergers of all kinds	Market portfolio
Asquith, Bruner, & Mullings, Jr.	1963–79 (USA)		0.028* (m = 0)		0.175*	214 early mergers by firms beginning	Market portfolio

TABLE VIII (Continued)

Study	Time period (country)	Returns prior to merger announcement, acquiring firms	Returns in announcement day (d) month (m), year (y) acquiring firm	Post-merger returns in days (d), months (m), years (y) after merger acquiring firms[a]	Acquired firms' returns	Sample	Control group
(1983)						merger programs after 1963	
Bradley, Desai, & Kim (1983)	1962–80 (USA)		0.024^* (m = 0)		0.318^*	161 successful tender offers	Market portfolio
Malatesta (1983)	1969–74 (USA)	0.043^* (m = −60, −1)	0.009 (m = 0)	-0.079^* (m = 1, 12)	0.168^*	256 mergers of all kinds	Market portfolio
Magenheim & Mueller (forthcoming)	1976–81 (USA)	0.184^* (m = −24, −4)	-0.003 (m = 0)	-0.422 (m = −3, 36)		78 mergers of all kinds	Market portfolio

Notes: Returns are measured between merging companies' returns and control group returns in all cases. In those studies in which the data were centered around the data of final consummation, the series were displaced backwards by 6 months to allow for the fact that announcements generally precede mergers by 6 months.

[a] Post-merger returns include gains (losses) in announcement day (d), month (m), or year (y) whenever possible.

[b] Reported data do not allow calculation of statistical significance.

[c] Month 0 in the Ellert study is the month in which a complaint is filed.

[d] Announcement of merger in Ellert study is measured as period from judicial complaint through settlement.

[e] Halpern's figures for acquiring firms are for largest of two companies involved in a merger. Acquired firms' figures are for the smallest of the two merging firms.

[f] Dodd reports figure for 10 days before announcement until 10 days after merger is approved. Calculation based on assumption that there are on average 6 months (26 weeks times 5 working days) between a merger's announcement and its approval.

facilitate comparisons, I have computed returns for both acquiring and acquired firms as the differences between merging company returns and control group returns. Thus, for example, the returns for the 43 nonconglomerate companies that engaged in heavy merger activity over the 1953–64 period which Hogarty (1970b) studied, average 5 percentage points lower than the industries in which they were based.

The easiest results to interpret are those for the acquired firms. The returns on their shares rise sharply at the time the mergers are announced; occasionally this rise commences one or two months prior to announcement. The average time span between announcement and completion of the merger is six months. When the merger is completed, the acquired firm disappears. The gains to acquired firm shareholders over this short period are positive and large. The median gain for the studies surveyed in Table VIII is 0.187.

More difficult to interpret are the results for the acquiring firms. In part, this difficulty arises because the acquiring firms do not disappear when the merger is completed. Thus, the question arises with respect to acquiring firms as to what period of time is appropriate to measure the *effects* of the mergers as reflected in shareholder returns.

Table VIII divides the shareholder returns' results for acquiring firms into three time periods: a period prior to the merger, ending in the month or year before the announcement the period immediately surrounding the merger or its announcement, and a post-merger period. Once the data are arrayed in this manner, a fairly uniform pattern actually does emerge across the several studies.

Perhaps the easiest way to illustrate this pattern is to consider first the results of a single study that typifies the others. Figure 2 presents a plot of the cumulative residuals used to compute shareholder returns for acquiring firms in the Dodd and Ruback (1977).[48] Time is in months measured on the horizontal axis. The residuals are obtained from a regression of acquiring firm returns on

---

[48] These were calculated by adding the monthly averages Dodd and Ruback (1977) report in their Table II (pp. 364–6). My cumulative totals differ trivially from theirs, e.g. between months +1 and +12, I obtain a −1.22 decline in return for successful bidders they report −1.32. A comparison of this figure and their Figure 2 (p. 363) yields the same visual impression.

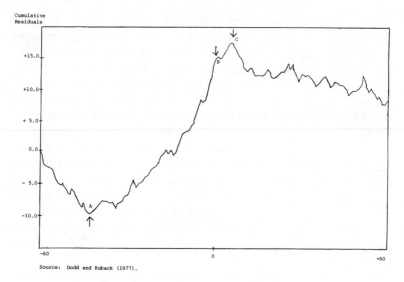

Source: Dodd and Ruback (1977).

FIGURE 2   Plots of cumulative residuals for successful bidding firms.

the market portfolio's return, and are centered around the merger announcement month. In the absence of new information about the firm's future performance, the expected value for the cumulative residuals series is zero. Sustained movements of the cumulative residuals series in an upward (downward) direction are presumed to signify the stock market's reaction to favorable (unfavorable) information about the firm's future performance.

There are three distinct movements in the cumulative residual series: an initial decline to A, a long, sustained rise from A to C, a gradual decline commencing at C and continuing until the data stop. Point A precedes the announcements of the mergers by 43 months. The rise in returns starting at A can hardly reflect the news of the merger reaching the market at B. If the rise between A and B is causally related to the mergers at all, it must be the increases in acquiring company returns that causes the managers of these companies to undertake mergers at this time.

The announcement of the merger at point B is accompanied by no visual market reaction. There is a positive gain to the shareholders of the acquiring firms in the month the mergers were announced, but so too were there consistent gains to these shareholders over the $3\frac{1}{2}$ years preceding the merger.

News that the mergers announced at B are definitely to take place reaches the market on average around point C. This information, in contrast to the announced intention to merge at B, does precipitate a visible reaction in the market. The rise in returns the acquiring firm shareholders had experienced over the 50 preceding months comes to a halt. A steady decline in shareholder returns occurs from C to the end of the time period studied. Between C and the last month recorded, shareholders of acquiring firms experience an 0.085 percentage point decline in returns.

The pattern of returns to acquiring company shareholders apparent in the Dodd and Ruback study—a sustained and substantial rise prior to the merger, a mixed immediate reaction to the merger, a decline in returns following the merger—reoccurs with some exceptions throughout the 22 studies included in Table VIII. Eleven of the twelve studies that report on the period prior to the mergers found positive, abnormal returns to acquiring firm shareholders. The one exception is the Franks, *et al.* (1977) study of UK brewers and distillers, but even they found that the brewing and distilling industry from which their entire sample was drawn was earning above normal returns in the pre-merger period. Both other UK studies and all eight US studies found positive acquiring firms' returns over long intervals preceding the mergers. Moreover, the magnitudes of the increases in abnormal returns are substantial. The median increase is 0.124.

In contrast, the median increase in shareholder returns around the time of the merger is only 0.009. The mergers come during a long time span in which acquiring firm shareholders are doing quite well, but the mergers themselves do not result in much of an improvement in shareholder returns. Following the mergers, a majority of the studies (14 of 19) report declines in returns. The median post-merger decline is −0.05.

The main issue, of course, is what the total effect upon acquiring firm shareholders has been. This question is difficult to answer for two reasons: First, since the mergers occur during (or more accurately at the end of) a long period of return increases, it is not clear whether those increases observed at the time mergers occur reflect the market's response to the mergers, or the mere continuance of the existing trend. Second, while the decline in returns following the mergers does appear to have been precipitated by them, it is not evident how long after the mergers one must track them to measure their full effect.

In addition to Dodd and Ruback, several other studies have observed continuous declines in acquiring company returns throughout the entire post-merger period investigated, e.g. Mandelker (1974), Langetieg (1978), Jenny and Weber (1980), Cosh, *et al.* (1980), and Mueller (1980). Given the consistency of this pattern, and the ambiguity of any increases observed coincident with the mergers, it would be rash to form a judgement on the anticipated effects of the mergers on the basis of evidence of returns only at the time of the merger. This reasoning suggests that a prudent estimate of the market's expectation of the effect of the mergers on acquiring firms be formed by adding the returns figures for the announcement period (month, year) to those for the post-merger period, omitting those studies (Halpern, 1973; Asquith, *et al.,* 1983; Bradley, *et al.,* 1983), which did not report post-merger returns, as well as those reporting on but a couple of months after the merger announcements (Bradley, 1980; Franks, *et al.,* 1976). Of the remaining 17 studies, 12 have negative returns to acquiring firm shareholders over the combined announcement period and post-merger interval. The median of these returns is -0.034.

b. *An interpretation.* The motives for mergers are many, and no single explanation can explain all. An eclectic posture, as Steiner (1975, pp. 180–4) adopts, is the most prudent. Yet, the pattern of results observed above is broadly consistent with the view that managers undertake acquisitions to maintain or increase the size of their firms, in spite of incurring transaction costs and other inefficiencies that lower company returns. To acquire another firm, a cash offer for shares must be made and/or an exchange of stock or debt. The most propitious time to undertake an acquisition is thus when one's cash flow and/or stock price is abnormally high. The timing of acquisitions at the end of sustained periods of abnormal positive returns for the acquiring firms is, thus, fully consistent with the hypothesis that mergers occur not out of the recognition of some synergy between acquirer and acquiree, since such recognition presumably can occur at any time, but out of enhanced capacity of firms to expand at certain points in time.

That the mergers do not bring about synergistic gains is indicated by the negative returns observed in 12 of the 17 studies that report both announcement period and post-merger returns. That these losses to acquiring firm shareholders are small in percentage terms does not diminish their economic importance for either the theory of the firm, or public policy. If management persists in undertaking acquisitions with negative mean returns, then some motive other than stockholder welfare must be driving their decisions.

If we assume that the combined market values of the acquiring and acquired companies reflect the market's estimation of the future returns of the combined enterprise, then for public policy purposes the relevant question is whether the combined impact of the mergers on share returns is positive or negative. To make this calculation, one must take into account the different relative sizes of the acquiring and acquired firms. Unfortunately, none of the studies report these data even as averages, and only a couple attempt the calculation themselves (e.g., Halpern, 1973; Firth, 1980). In my study, acquiring companies averaged ten times the size of acquirees. Thus, to compare acquiring company returns with those of their acquirees, the former would have to be scaled by a factor of 10. This would make the median acquiring firm return in Table VIII −0.34, which roughly doubles the positive 0.187 median return of the acquired company shareholders. While such a calculation is admittedly rough, it does serve to highlight the fact that too much weight should not be given to the large positive returns of the acquired firms in judging the total effects of the mergers. The effect of the mergers on acquired firm returns is certain; once the merger goes through, it is the premium above premerger market price. Since the gain is concentrated in a period of a few months, it is easy to measure and of necessity positive and significant. In contrast, the effect of the mergers on the acquiring companies' share prices reflects the market's appraisal of the future impact of the merger. When the market's reaction is drawn out over a long stretch of time, and the acquired firm is small relative to the acquirer, the measured effect on the acquiring firm's shareholders is small of necessity and diffcult to disentangle from other events. This problem is particularly likely when, as seems to be the case, the mergers come upon an independent, upward trend in acquiring firm returns.

In this regard, some additional results of Malatesta (1983) are revealing. He found that the larger firms in his sample actually experienced slightly positive, post-merger returns (0.045 over the 12 months subsequent to the merger's announcement). But the smaller acquiring firms experienced relatively larger, negative returns, −0.077. The acquired companies are, of course, likely to be larger relative to small acquiring firms than they are to large ones. The returns for small acquiring firms after a merger are more likely to reflect the market's appraisal of the mergers' effects than are the returns for larger acquirers for which the mergers will get less weight. Yet the greater relative importance of the mergers results in a larger relative loss to acquiring firm shareholders.

c. *Contrast with other interpretations.* The interpretation of the evidence on mergers' effects on shareholder returns given here differs from what several other reviewers of this literature have reached.[49] Since the issue is crucial to understanding and appraising the evolutionary course of Western capitalism, a discussion of the reasoning behind the more favorable interpretations of the evidence is in order.

Both sides agree that acquired company shareholders are better off, so the differences boil down to differences over the effects of mergers on acquiring company shareholders. Perhaps the best way to proceed is to return again to the Dodd and Ruback study. When I look at the data in Figure 2, I see a long rise in returns to acquiring firm shareholders that certainly could not have been caused by the mergers and probably was a cause of the tender offers. There is no apparent break in the upward trend in acquiring firm returns at the time they are announced. The increase in acquiring firm returns in the month the merger is announced (point B), and over the subsequent six months can as easily be interpreted as an extension of the trend which started 43 months earlier, as it can as a result of the announcement. The fact that this upward trend breaks at the time the mergers take place (*C*) and a sustained decline sets in thereafter strikes me as more than a coincidence. I

---

[49] See Brozen (1982), Benston (1980), Jensen and Ruback (1983), and Halpern (1983). Three other observers have surveyed the same terrain and arrived at conclusions more akin to mine, Steiner (1975, ch. 8), Scherer (1980, pp. 138–41), Rhoades (1983). That all of those giving mergers mixed reviews are industrial organization economists, while those according them rave reviews are housed in American Business Schools is but one of many curiosa in this literature.

attribute the decline in returns until the end of the sample period to the mergers.

When Dodd and Ruback look at the same data, they conclude that "[t]his evidence is consistent with gains from takeovers to stockholders of successful bidding firms . . . " (1977, p. 369). How is this conclusion attained? First, Dodd and Ruback ignore the long run up in returns that precedes the tender offers (or possibly misinterpret them as part of the gains to bidding firm shareholders *from* the mergers. See last paragraph, 5.2.1, p. 369). They do so in spite of the fact that the increase in returns that precedes the announcement, 0.117, is far greater than any changes occurring around the announcement and when the relative size of the acquiring and acquired firms is considered, is far greater than the gains to acquired company shareholders. The rise in returns to acquiring firm shareholders in the 43 months preceding the take-overs is the single, economically most important change in asset values in the Dodd and Ruback results, yet they do not discuss it. They view mergers as improving the internal efficiency of the acquired firms, and since this hypothesis does not imply any movement in acquiring firm share prices prior to an acquisition, that which is there is ignored.[50] Given that the acquiring firms' return increases preceding the merger are ignored, the possibility that the increase in returns at the time of the announcement might be part of an ongoing trend is also not considered. Thus, the increase in returns to acquiring firm shareholders in the month of the announcement is attributed entirely to the merger announcement.

Dodd and Ruback conclude that the tender offers have had a positive impact, because of a statistically significant increase in the average residuals in the month the offers are made.[51] But this

---

[50] Their hypothesis does suggest that acquired company returns may decline prior to takeover and this is examined. Unlike some studies they do *not* find below normal returns for acquired firm shareholders prior to the takeover. Thus, if the target firms were inefficiently managed, the market did not perceive this prior to their disappearance.

[51] They switch at month zero from calculating residuals from estimates of the characteristic line based on the period $[-74, -14]$ to estimates from $[+14, +74]$. The former period includes some of the above normal premerger returns, the latter overlaps substantially with the post-merger decline. Thus, Dodd and Ruback switch at month 0 to using a benchmark of lower performance to predict acquiring firm returns and this change in benchmarks probably explains some of the above "normal" returns recorded in month 0. For further discussion of this point, see Magenheim and Mueller (forthcoming).

increase is only 2.83 percent, less than half of the fall in returns of 5.91 that occurs over the next 60 months. Thus, a shareholder who bought an acquiring firm's shares just prior to the merger announcement and held the shares over the next five years experienced a more than three percentage point decline relative to what one would predict from movements in the market portfolio. Moreover, if the shareholder were unlucky enough to buy an acquiring firm's shares in the month when the mergers were completed, he would suffer a loss of almost 8.5 percentage points.[52]

The reasoning by which Dodd and Ruback conclude that acquiring firm shareholders are made better off from acquisitions from results as depicted in Figure 2 resembles the reasoning underlying other studies, which reach this conclusion. The presumption is that the merger takes place to achieve some synergy between the acquiring and acquired companies, or more often that it is some failing on the part of the acquired company's management that elicits the bid. Thus, attention to premerger performance is centered on the acquired company's performance. The substantial increases in acquiring firm returns prior to the mergers are ignored, as are the hypotheses that might reverse the causal link, by implying that the acquiring firm's above normal performance enables them to make the acquisition. Since the premerger increases in acquiring firm returns are ignored, so too is the possibility that any increases in returns observed at the merger's announcement are not a result of the announcement but a continuation of the existing trend. The efficient-market assumption is used to justify devoting exclusive attention to gains and losses immediately surrounding the merger's announcements. The declines in acquiring firm returns that typically follow the merger announcements are ignored. Five of the studies from Table VIII, which conclude mergers improve efficiency, examine the acquiring firms' returns for no longer than 2 months after merger. If these returns are negative but insignificantly different

---

[52] Dodd and Ruback do not report whether this substantial decline from C to the end of the period is statistically significant, nor whether the 5.91 percentage point decline from B to the sample period's end is. One cannot determine without the original data whether these declines are statistically significant, but whether they are or are not is irrelevant for the conclusion that shareholders of acquiring firms who retain their shares well beyond the immediate announcement month are *not* better off than they would have been in the absence of the mergers.

from zero, *they are treated as if they were zero,* even when the relative size of the acquiring firms is so large that the acquiring firms losses are more than enough to negate the gains to the much smaller target firms.

The issue of whether mergers do tend to improve economic efficiency on average is central to an evaluation of competing theories of the firm, and to an evaluation of the overall performance of corporate capitalism as it functions today. Given the importance of the issue, it is a pity that a consensus among observers of mergers does not exist. But it does not. Thus, I have had to take the reader into the quagmire, that constitutes the empirical literature on returns to merging firms' shareholders. We have now waded around in this segment of the story enough for the reader to have gained a reasonable impression of what the results look like, and why there exists disagreement over their implications. Let us move on.

I. The stages of development of corporate capitalism

The pattern of evolution for the individual corporation, which has been described in broad outline parallels the pattern of development of corporate capitalism over the past century at least within the United Kingdom and the United States. Leslie Hannah for the UK (1976) and Alfred D. Chandler, Jr., for the USA (1962) both describe the pattern of corporate development in their respective countries since 1850 in terms of stages or phases of development that parallel the stages of a firm's development described here. The patterns of development within the two countries also roughly parallel one another.

Both Hannah and Chandler describe the first phase of corporate capitalism as culminating at the First World War (Hannah, 1976, ch. 2; Chandler, 1962, pp. 386–7). Markets grew rapidly during the latter half of the 19th century, particularly in the United States where the extension of the railroad connected East and West and created large markets for existing and new products. Firms also grew rapidly, but so rapid was the growth in market size that at least in the UK, there were still few relatively large companies at the turn of the century (Hannah, 1976, p. 10). Both countries experienced a merger wave at the close of the century coinciding with a boom in stock market prices. The merger wave in the

United States was of much greater dimensions than in Great Britain and this helped produce a greater number of very large companies in the United States than in the United Kingdom (Hannah, 1976, p. 24). In both countries, these mergers were largely horizontal or horizontal/vertical in nature, so that in the United States this first great merger wave resulted in an unprecedented number of large, dominant firms.[53]

At the end of the first phase of corporate capitalism's development, most firms were family firms of one form or another, still led by their entrepreneurial creators. Firm and individual names were linked. Swift in meatpacking, Duke in cigarettes (to become American Tobacco upon the acquisition of several firms at the end of the century), McCormick in agricultural products, Carnegie in steel until its absorption into United States Steel, and du Pont in chemicals. In Great Britain, partnerships and family firms predominated and even the three largest companies at the end of the period—J. & P. Coats, Imperial Tobacco, and Watney Combe Reid—were built up "around old family firms with their senior management and directors recruited principally from among the founding families" (Hannah, 1976, p. 26).

On the other hand, at the end of the 19th century, several companies did grow and mature sufficiently rapidly so that they took on many of the characteristics of the large, mature corporation, as, for example, a separation of ownership from control.[54] Most conspicuous among these early giants in both America and the United Kingdom were the railroads. The following statement by the Board of Directors of the Pennsylvania Railroad in 1874 reads as if it were taken from Berle and Means's book published a half century later.

> The present form of organisation (part-time directors and full-time officers) makes practical ciphers of the Directors, and this is from no deliberate intention, but from the very necessities of the case. Once a large business had reached a size that required the services of several full-time administrators, the board and the stockholders had only a negative or *veto* power on the government of their enterprise and on the allocation of its resources. They could say no, but they had neither

---

[53] Markham (1955), Nelson (1959), Reid (1968, ch. 3).

[54] See Hannah (1976, p. 12) and references cited there in footnote 10.

the information nor the awareness of the company's situation to propose realistic alternative courses of action [taken from Chandler (1962, p. 313)].

Neither the ability nor the inclination of most members of the Board of Directors to police management has changed much in the 111 years since the statement was made. Corporate raider Carl Icahn's observations have an even more pessimistic ring.

> You get there [to a board meeting] early in the morning, and everybody is reading the newspaper. The first thing is that everybody looks at their check, puts it in their pocket, smiles big, and then goes back to reading the newspaper.
>
> The meeting starts, you get the room dark and a few guys go to sleep. Then they put a slide machine up with a lot of numbers that even Einstein wouldn't understand.
>
> The CEO doesn't even do it. He gets some financial guy to show all these numbers. And then everybody is reading the newspaper anyway, or when it is dark they are sleeping.
>
> I was on one board and this went on for a while. I had no inside information being on that board because I couldn't figure out what they were doing. And that is the truth if there ever was truth. (*Washington Post,* May 19, 1985, p. H3)

The first phase of corporate capitalism's development was followed by a period of rationalization in both the United Kingdom and the United States. Although the timing of this second phase of development as it is recorded by Hannah and Chandler differs somewhat between the two countries, both authors use the word "rationalization" to describe a period of roughly 20 years in duration at the beginning of this century.

Following a brief boom shortly after World War I, Britain entered into an economic slump that continued until World War II broke out. The dismal performance of the British economy during this period resulted in increasing disenchantment with the working of the market. The socialist movement favoring greater government intervention was the left wing's response to this disenchantment. The rationalization movement was the response of the right. Inadequacies in the market mechanism would be offset by larger, more efficient companies, which could reap the benefits of scale economies and the newly emerging scientific management techniques. These claims led to demands for still more horizontal and vertical acquisitions, and to the government's allowing various cooperative or cartel-like agreements among firms. Once again, concentration levels rose in the United Kingdom. This rise coincided with another wave of mergers, and appears to have been caused by it.[55]

Chandler puts the rationalization period in the United States between 1900 and 1920, and describes it mainly as one of organizational changes to formalize communication channels in the giant firms that were necessitated by the rapid growth at the end of the 19th century and the turn-of-the-century merger wave (Chandler, 1962, p. 384, ff.). But mergers also occurred in this country, with a second great wave taking place during the twenties, and concentration levels were pushed upward in several industries (Stigler, 1950; Reid, 1968, ch. 4).

While the first phase of corporate capitalism's development was carried out by "the empire builders of American industry," the task of organizing these giants in such a way to allow their managers to control and monitor these empires effectively was turned over to individuals from outside of the founding families (Chandler, 1962, pp. 387–8). The separation of ownership from control, visible in a few companies before 1900, became a reality in many, in the first 30 years of this century as Berle and Means (1932) documented in their famous book.

Corporate expansion in the first two stages of capitalism's development was largely within initial product lines (horizontal growth), or into markets that are either vertically linked to the firm's initial products, or natural extensions of these products based on marketing or technological complementarities. Stage three is one of increased emphasis upon diversification. While some examples of companies, which entered into their diversification phases as early as the 1920s can be found, e.g. GE and du Pont in the United States, GEC and Imperial Chemical in the United Kingdom, for most companies diversification became an important growth strat-

---

[55] Hannah (1976, ch. 3). With respect to the specific question of mergers and concentration in the United Kingdom, see also Hannah and Kay (1977), and for an alternative view Hart and Prais (1956) and Singh (1971).

egy only following World War II. Hannah for example, cites figures for a sample of large United Kingdom firms indicating a steady rise in the percentage one can classify as diversified from 25 percent in 1950 to 45 percent in 1960, to 60 percent in 1970 (Hannah, 1976, p. 174). Once again, mergers have played a major role in the process of corporate growth during this stage.

In part, because the passage of the Celler–Kefauver Amendment to Section 7 of the Clayton Act in 1950 significantly curtailed opportunities for horizontal and vertical mergers in the United States, the process of diversification has gone much faster and further in the United States than in the United Kingdom and other European countries. Thus, today the firm Augustus Swift founded a century ago to pack meat and ship it from the Midwest to Eastern markets neither bears his name nor packs meat. Its vestige survives as subsidiary in the giant Beatrice empire. The trend in this country is for companies to adopt new names that symbolically sever ties with the names of both the founding entrepreneur and the product upon which the firm's success was initially based.

The list of the 200 largest companies in the United States today is filled by firms, each of which produces a wide spectrum of products, most of which are managed by individuals who own a modest fraction of the company's outstanding shares. These managers typically have neither experience nor expertise regarding the production and marketing of the many products their firm sells. Lacking knowledge and loyalty to any given product or product line, they add and delete product lines from their portfolio of divisions at a remarkable rate. The giant corporation of today is one whose abstract alphabetical name neither reveals the persons and products of its past, nor presages those of its future.

Alongside these amorphous giants, new companies continue to come into existence and set off upon the path of corporate maturation. Most disappear quickly. Some survive the early shake-out period only to be acquired while they are still relatively young and strong. A few will develop into one of the diversified giants of tomorrow. Thus, while it is natural to characterize corporate capitalism today by the largest of its representatives, the giant, mature, diversified companies, there nevertheless exist at the same time examples of companies in all stages of corporate development.

Part III

BEYOND MANAGERIAL CAPITALISM

No one placed greater emphasis on the evolutionary character of capitalism than Karl Marx. Yet, a century after Marx predicted its evolutionary demise, capitalism still lives in most of the lands where it once took root.

Although alive, capitalism is not necessarily well in each of the countries. Great Britain, the cradle of capitalism as well as Adam Smith's homeland, falls further and further behind its capitalist sisters by every definition of economic efficiency. On the European continent, each post-World War II miracle has in varying degrees become an unhappy reality of high unemployment, slow productivity growth, and the loss of markets to Asian competitors. Pessimism regarding Europe's future ability to compete in world markets abounds.

In North America the objective situation is not much different. The current recovery ends a decade of stagnation, but productivity increases have not regained earlier levels and unemployment remains higher than it was for a generation after World War II. One market after another is lost to foreign competition.

Are these passing phases in capitalism's development, as perhaps the thirties was, to be followed by a new burst of growth and development, or are they symptomatic of more fundamental problems inherent in modern, managerial capitalism? If the latter, does the material of Part II shed light on the nature of these problems and possible remedies?

Definitive answers to these questions are obviously impossible to give. But I believe the characteristics of managerial capitalism described above do provide some insight to what has been happening. When Schumpeter first outlined the salient characteristics of capitalism at the beginning of the twentieth century, there was but one way to construct a "private kingdom." One had to build it from the bottom up. This option still exists today, but now there is a second route to the top of a corporate empire, climb the hierarchical ladder within an existing giant. One of Marx's other famous predictions has come true. Control of industrial assets has become more and more concentrated in corporate hands. Those who succeed in reaching the top of a giant corporate hierarchy command an organization, which they could never hope to build in their own lifetime. Many of those who strove a century ago to build their own businesses strive today to get ahead in businesses others have built, or, increasingly, to take over an ongoing enterprise.

A century ago most great fortunes were made by those who founded and built the first generation of corporate giants. But even then there was opportunity for some to get ahead simply by helping to put the great trusts together. Both the Mellons and the Carnegies grew wealthy during the first merger movement. Promoters profits have since the first great merger movement received a place of prominence in any list of causes for mergers (Stigler, 1950; Markham, 1955). They remain an important contributing factor. Today an industry of investment bankers, consultants and lawyers exists to facilitate and encourage the merger process.

Increases in the market values of target firms of 50 percent are commonplace today, 100 percent premia are not rare. Substantial gains are possible and fortunes can and are made overnight. The development of the modern stock, bond, commodity and foreign exchange markets has given those with a penchant for plunging alternative options for making a quick fortune. Risk-taking today often consists of speculation on changes in asset values rather than on one's ability to create asset value. It may be coincidence that the two Western Nations with the most highly developed capital markets and most active markets for corporate control have had the slowest economic growth since World War II. But this essay has reviewed evidence suggesting why these phenomena may be causally related.

Having constructed this essay around an evolutionary theme, it would be malapropos simply to end without casting at least a glance at what the next phase of managerial capitalism might be or what lies beyond it. Economists are remarkably bad at forecasting next quarter's GNP, next year's inflation rate. It would be foolhardy to try to forecast capitalism's course over the next century. Instead, I shall sketch what appear to be the most plausible options. The discussion is inherently speculative.

J. The continuance of managerial capitalism

The most obvious and likely next phase of managerial capitalism is a simple extrapolation of the existing phase. Despite its inefficiencies, the "inherent contradictions" of managerial capitalism are not so severe as to make its demise inevitable. The inherently decentralized nature of a market economy combined with its reliance on individual initiative spurred by the desire for private gain result in the continual emergence of small and medium-sized firms alongside the giants. These enterprises fill the interstices the giants leave, help maintain the efficiency of the giant corporations by providing alternatives for both buyers and factor owners, and perhaps most importantly, provide a potential outlet for those iconoclastic and innovative individuals whose initiative would be suppressed in the large, bureaucratic corporation. Their acquisition provides the sustenance through with the giant firms maintain their size and growth. Capitalism has survived to the end of the twentieth century because it is sufficiently flexible to allow and encourage the creation of organizations and institutions for mitigating its mistakes.

The market for corporate control may yet develop into an institution capable of correcting some of the inefficiencies stemming from the principal-agent problem. While until recently acquisitions have seemed more symptomatic of the problem, as large mature corporations absorbed smaller ones with impunity, in the last decade in the United States the small have begun to prey upon the large. Size no longer can protect a management whose company's share price falls sufficiently far so that an attacker can borrow against the assets of the firm to finance the takeover bid, sell off enough of the assets after the takeover to pay back the loan, and still have enough left over to constitute a tidy profit. That opportunities such as these exist in substantial numbers is as clear evidence in favor of the proposition that managers overinvest and overexpand as any other fact.

One of the responses of managers to the attacks of the takeover raiders has been to buy back large quantities of outstanding shares and replace them with debt or in some cases "super shares" carrying multiple votes. These strategems help to protect management from takeovers by concentrating voting power in their hands.

Thus, one of the responses of "the market" to the excesses of growth, diversification and acquisitions that the separation of ownership from control furthers has been to reconcentrate ownership with control. In this way, capitalism often does tend to correct for its own excesses.

Even if these developments prove to be incapable of fully eliminating the excesses and inefficiencies of managerial capitalism, the differences in static and dynamic efficiency between the maturing economies of North America and Europe and the emerging economies of Asia and some other parts of the world may not force a radical shift in structure in the former. Absolute levels of income are very high in Europe and North America by world standards and if they should not increase as rapidly as they could or as they do in other parts of the world, discontent may still not become so great that any radical restructuring of capitalist institutions is undertaken. The most likely future course of managerial capitalism in the West sees the large corporation as the most prominant economic actor with giant corporations coming to dominate the service, retailing and other sectors once populated by small firms. Arbitrage markets continue their evolutionary growth affording the daring opportunities for quick gain. Predicting asset value changes continues to draw scarce entrepreneurial energy away from creating asset values. But enough "old fashioned" entrepreneurs are left to start up new firms and resuscitate old ones so that innovations and productivity increases continue in the West, if at an attenuated pace. The "British disease" continues its advance across the Western capitalist economies, but does not prove fatal in most cases.

K. The Japanese alternative

Marx argued that capitalism was so exploitative that the workers would one day rise up and replace it with a socialist system. But the forms of socialism, which have been practiced in Marx's name, are so inefficient in satisfying the workers' needs as consumers while not being obviously less repressive of the individual as worker that no country has ever voluntarily switched in toto from a capitalist to a socialist system. Even "creeping socialism" has crept to a halt.

Instead of succumbing to the charms of socialism, mature

capitalist nations are succumbed by the brash competitive force of newly emerging capitalist nations. First, Great Britian, then the United States, and now Japan have stepped forward to assume the position of leading capitalist nation.

So swift has been the rise of the Japanese economy and so different seems the Japanese form of corporate capitalism from that predominating in North America that many have tried to explain Japan's success by pointing to certain aspects of Japanese institutional and organizational structures that differ from those found in Europe and North America. But striking too are the parallels.

Rather distinct phases in the development of capitalism in Japan can be observed.[56] The Meiji Restoration ushered in an era of entrepreneurial capitalism in Japan which Hirschmeier and Yui (1981) place in the period 1868–95. The ideas of the enlightenment took some root during this period. They did not fully displace Japan's traditional emphasis on the family and on the individual's obligation to family, community and nation, but they did make understandable if not quite respectable the assertion of individual initiative which is required for capitalism to supplant feudalism. Writers, such as Fukuzawa Yukichi, extolled profits maximization as a necessary complement to Japan's emergence from feudalism. This period witnessed the birth of numerous important companies in railways, mining, and banking just as occurred in the Western capitalist countries at this time.

Following this early entrepreneurial period, Japan entered a long phase of development in which the great zaibatsu emerged. These giant conglomerates of financial and industrial activity became symbols of Japanese capitalism up until World War II. Visible during the years between 1896 and 1945 was the gradual replacement of apprentice-managers lacking in formal education by college graduates. The families, which founded the enterprises, retreated as college-trained "professional" managers took over. The cost-cutting specialist rose to power. Production was rationalized (Hirschmeier and Yui, 1981, pp. 177–83). Gradually the separation of ownership from control appeared (Hirschmeier and Yui, 1981, pp. 196–7). Boards of directors no longer controlled management, but rather were absorbed into it (pp. 199–200). Still, prior to World War II the

---

[56] See in particular the discussion in Hirschmeier and Yui (1981).

original ties between company and founding family were often visible. Top management continued to own large fractions of their company's shares in many cases and/or received large bonuses when profits were high. Thus, up through World War II, profits maximization was the primary objective of most large and small Japanese firms.

The zaibatsu were dismembered following World War II only to reassemble as the gigantic conglomerate groups so visible around the world today. But one consequence of the dissolution of the zaibatsu did not get reversed. The lingering ties with the founding families, which still existed with the zaibatsu, were severed. Ownership became completely separated from management in the large diversified Japanese firm, with the predictable consequence, that "economic growth and expansion of market shares became the top goals . . . of the postwar business leadership."[57] Thus, in terms of both its current size, structure and managerial objectives, and its historical evolution, the modern Japanese corporation resembles in many ways its Western counterpart.

Yet there are important differences between the two. In going from feudalism to advanced, industrial capitalism in little more than a century Japan has been able to retain certain elements of its past culture to a greater extent than the developed countries of North America and Europe. The institution of the family remains strong and the company has replaced the village as the community beyond the family to which ones moral obligations belong. Economic stability is provided to the Japanese worker through lifetime contracts and the seniority-determined wage increases characteristic of the large firms. These companies often provide their employees housing and recreational facilities also. Thus, the Japanese worker's life revolves around his company to a much greater extent than in the West. The Japanese sense of loyalty and obligation to community has to a considerable degree been transferred to the employer. The consequence is the spectacular differences between Japan and the Western nations in hours worked, vacation days, productivity increases, and the like.

While it is unlikely that Western corporations could ever induce the sense of community and loyalty among their employees that is

---

[57] Hirschmeier and Yui (1981, p. 315). See also Nanto (1982), p. 12.

possible in Japan, certain elements of the Japanese industrial organization system could conceivably be adopted with beneficial consequences. The Japanese emphasis on treating the firm as a community, as a "second family," naturally carries with it a greater emphasis on human relations in the Japanese firm than occurs in the more impersonal environment of the Western corporation. Japanese scholars stress the importance of the firm as an internal labor market (Itami, 1985, p. 72) just as Western scholars emphasize the functioning of the large corporation as an internal capital market (Williamson, 1975). In the West, managers place great emphasis on the allocation of internal fund flows to finance investment and rely to a greater extent on external markets for labor, even at upper managerial levels. In Japan, it is the internal labor market that commands management's primary attention, capital being more heavily obtained from external markets (Itami, 1985, pp. 71–2). Diversification and spin-offs are decisions in Japan that are made from the bottom up and are often motivated to better utilize the work force and expertise of the firm or to harmonize work and promotion schedules. In contrast, diversification decisions are dominated in the United States by capital considerations.[58] As Thurow (1985, pp. 119–21) notes, internal expansion is a more natural route to diversification when diversification results from lower level suggestions for the better utilization of existing personnel and capital. Mergers are a more natural route to diversification when decisions come from a top management seeking a more efficient use of capital.

It is, of course, possible to envisage Western corporations adopting Japanese practices: a greater attention to labor relations, greater job security, greater employee participation in profit and control sharing, more reliance on internal than external (merger) growth. But existing institutional structures in the West do not seem conducive to such changes. Managerial salaries are higher by several orders of magnitude in Western companies than they are in their Japanese counterparts. Western managers change jobs more frequently and use the threat of changing jobs as a means of increasing their incomes. "Idemitsu Sazo, founder of Idemitsu

---

[58] See Hattori's discussion of Seiko's diversification (1985) as well as Aoki (1984, pp. 26–31) and Itami (1985, pp. 73–75).

Kosan, wrote the following comment on this system: 'The essential difference between an American company and Idemitsu is this: in America, able managers are baited with high salaries like fish and change from one company to another. In Japan such a man would be considered a traitor and an immoral and mean fellow'" (Hirschmeier and Yui, 1981, p. 348).

Moreover, the lack of identification of employee with employing organization is reinforced by the increasing tendency for companies or parts thereof to be bought and sold in the market for corporate control. What incentive does a blue collar worker or division manager have to be loyal to the parent firm when he or she knows that the parent stands ready to divest the division or disband it should its operating performance falter? The extension of takeover activity to the largest companies extends this short run orientation toward the company to the upper echelons of corporate management of the largest firms. A management preoccupied with the design of "golden parachutes" to protect it after it leaves the company cannot view its company's future with the same perspective as the Japanese manager whose departure from the firm occurs only upon his death or retirement.

Rather than moving in the direction of longer run ties between worker and company and greater employee-employer loyalty, developments in the West seem if anything to be moving toward shorter run, more impersonal relationships. If opportunistic behavior in an implicit contractual relationship is the opposite of loyal behavior, the West is moving away from the Japanese model, not toward it.

L. Final queries

The pace at which capitalist economies have changed since World War II is remarkable. The economies of Japan, Italy and West Germany were rebuilt in less than a generation. Europe successfully beat off the "American challenge" of the sixties only to succumb to the "Arab challenge" of the seventies and its demoralizing aftermath. Today both Europe and America struggle to ward off the "Japanese–Asian challenge."

What role will the large corporation play in this struggle? Will it solve its principal-agent inefficiencies by reuniting ownership and control? Will it shrink to a more efficient, innovative size by spinning off the extraneous operations previous generations of agents assembled? Or will it induce loyalty, innovativeness and risk-taking while maintaining size by transforming itself from a place of work into a community of workers, as capitalist reformers have urged since the birth of capitalism and as the Japanese practice today? The seeds for all three developments are planted; time and patience will reveal which take root.

References

Abernathy, William J., *The Productivity Dilemma,* Baltimore, Johns Hopkins University Press, 1978.

Amihud, Yakov and Baruch Lev, "Risk Reduction as a Managerial Motive for Conglomerate Mergers," *Bell Journal of Economics,* Autumn 1981, **12,** pp. 605–17.

Aoki, Masahiko, "Aspects of the Japanese Firm," in Masahiko Aoki, ed. *The Economic Analysis of the Japanese Firm,* North Holland: Amsterdam, 1984, pp. 3–43.

Arrow, Kenneth J., "The Economic Implications of Learning by Doing," *Review of Economic Studies,* June 1962, **29,** pp. 155–73.

Asquith, Paul, "Merger Bids, Uncertainty, and Stockholder Returns," *Journal of Financial Economics,* April 1983, **11,** pp. 51–83.

Asquith, Paul, Robert F. Bruner and David W. Mullins, Jr., "The Gains to Bidding Firms from Merger," *Journal of Financial Economics,* April 1983, **11,** pp. 121–39.

Azzi, Corry, "Conglomerate Mergers, Default Risk, and Homemade Mutual Funds," *American Economic Review,* March 1978, **68,** pp. 161–72.

Baumol, William J., P. Heim, B. G. Malkiel and R. E. Quandt, "Earnings Retention, New Capital and the Growth of the Firm," *Review of Economics and Statistics,* November 1970, **52,** pp. 345–55.

Baumol, William, J., P. Heim, B. G. Malkiel and R. E. Quandt, "Efficiency of Corporate Investment: Reply," *Review of Economics and Statistics,* February 1973, **55,** pp. 128–131.

Baumol, William J., John C. Panzar and Robert D. Willig, *Contestable Markets and the Theory of Industry Structure,* New York: Harcourt, Brace, and Jovanovich, 1982.

Beam, Henry, "The New Route to the Top," *Advanced Management Journal,* Spring 1979, **44,** pp. 55–62.

Bello, Francis, "The Year of the Transistor," *Fortune,* March 1953, **47,** p. 128ff.

Benston, George J., *Conglomerate Mergers,* Washington, D.C., American Enterprise Institute, 1980.

Berle, Adolf A. and Gardner C. Means, *The Modern Corporation and Private Property,* New York: Commerce Clearing House, 1932; rev. ed. New York: Harcourt, Brace, Jovanovich, 1968.

Berry, Charles H., *Corporate Growth and Diversification,* Princeton: Princeton University Press, 1975.

Boyle, Stanley E., *Conglomerate Merger Performance: An Empirical Analysis of Nine Corporations,* Washington, D.C.: Federal Trade Commission, 1972.

Bradley, Michael, "Interfirm Tender Offers and the Market for Corporate Control," *Journal of Business,* October 1980, **53,** pp. 345–76.

Bradley, Michael, Anand Desai and E. Han Kim, "The Rationale Behind Interfirm Tender Offers: Information or Synergy?" *Journal of Financial Economics,* April 1983, **11,** pp. 183–206.

Brainard, W. C., J. B. Shoven and L. Weiss, "The Financial Valuation of the Return on Capital," *Brookings Papers on Economic Activity,* **2,** 1980, pp. 453–502.

Brealey, R. A., S. D. Hodges and D. Capron, "The Return on Alternative Sources of Finance," *Review of Economics & Statistics,* November 1967, **58,** pp. 469–77.

Brenner, Menachem and David H. Downes, "A Critical Evaluation of the Measurement of Conglomerate Performance Using the Capital Asset Pricing Model," *Review of Economics and Statistics,* May 1979, **61,** pp. 292–96.

Brozen, Yale, *Concentration, Mergers and Public Policy,* New York: MacMillan, 1982.

Burns, Arthur F., *Production Trends in the United States Since 1870,* New York: National Bureau of Economic Research, 1934.

Business Week, "Why Litton Took a Slide," January 27, 1968, p. 38.

Business Week, "What Puts the Whiz in Litton's Fast Growth?" April 16, 1982, p. 180.

Buzzell, Robert D. and Robert Nourse, *Product Innovation, the Product Life Cycle, and Competitive Behavior in Selected Food Processing Industries,* Cambridge, Mass.: Arthur D. Little, 1966.

Calvo, Guillermo A. and Stanislaw Wellisz, "Supervision, Loss of Control, and the Optimum Size of the Firm," *Journal of Political Economy,* October 1978, **86,** pp. 943–52.

Camacho, Antonio and William D. White, "A Note on Loss of Control and the Optimum Size of the Firm," *Journal of Political Economy,* April 1981, **89,** pp. 407–10.

Carter, John R., "In Search of Synergy: A Structure-Performance Test," *Review of Economics and Statistics,* August 1977, **59,** pp. 279–89.

Caves, Richard E., "Corporate Strategy and Structure," *Journal of Law and Economics,* March 1980, **18,** pp. 64–92.

Caves, Richard E., Michael E. Porter, Michael Spence with John T. Scott, *Competition in the Open Economy,* Cambridge: Harvard University Press, 1980.

Caves, Richard E. and Basil S. Yamey, "Risk and Corporate Rates of Return: Comment," *Quarterly Journal of Economics,* August 1971, **85,** pp. 513–17.

Chandler, Alfred D., *Strategy and Structure,* Cambridge, Mass.: MIT Press, 1962.

Chandler, Alfred D., Jr., *The Visible Hand,* Cambridge, Mass.: Belknap Press, 1977.

Channon, Derek F., *The Strategy and Structure of British Enterprise,* Boston: Graduate School of Business Administration, Harvard University, 1973.

Cosh, Andrew, Alan Hughes and Ajit Singh, "The Causes and Effects of Takeovers in the United Kingdom: An Empirical Investigation for the Late 1960s at the Microeconomic Level," in Mueller (1980), pp. 227–70.

Cowling, K., P. Stoneman, J. Cubbin, J. Cable, G. Hall, S. Domberger and P. Dutton, *Mergers and Economic Performance,* Cambridge: Cambridge University Press, 1979.

Crum, W. L., *Corporate Size and Earning Power,* Cambridge, Mass.: Harvard University Press, 1939.